PRAISE FOR *THE GATHERING STORM*

"At the heart of Al Mohler's powerful new book is a fundamental truth: for all of us, what we believe profoundly influences the way we live. Most people of faith understand that argument, even while we try to ignore or dismiss the rise of militant, uncompromising secularism in every corner of our culture. Dr. Mohler shows the way that the undermining of religious values contributes to a host of acute national problems, from the beginning of life through its very end. *The Gathering Storm* offers a timely warning that can help Christians and their allies understand and overcome some of the menacing forces increasingly surrounding us."

—MICHAEL MEDVED, RADIO TALK SHOW HOST,
AUTHOR OF *GOD'S HAND ON AMERICA*

"In the midst of our cultural and moral decay, Albert Mohler stands as one of this generation's most incisive thinkers and articulate communicators. These gifts and more are on full display in *The Gathering Storm*. In this book Mohler triages the myriad challenges before contemporary Christians, and skillfully prescribes the most biblically faithful way forward. According to Mohler, these are not times for despair, but sober mindedness, conviction, and courage. I pray this book is widely read, and this message is well heeded."

—JASON K. ALLEN, PRESIDENT OF MIDWESTERN BAPTIST
THEOLOGICAL SEMINARY AND SPURGEON COLLEGE

"We who now live in the late modern age witness a great falling apart, a center that may not hold," warns Dr. Albert Mohler in his new book *The Gathering Storm*. Dr. Mohler is not an alarmist. So I say to you: If Al Mohler is worried, you should be worried. Very worried. This book is not a call to arms so much as a *cri de cœur* aimed at everyone who is not yet cut off from hearing an argument from the other side on anything. Mohler has surveyed the field of difficult issues and barely can find a hopeful sign. Again: Be worried. Be very worried. But don't be paralyzed. Read. Think. Pray. Start with this book and with everything Al Mohler has to say."

—HUGH HEWITT

"Speaking moral and spiritual truth to political, economic, and cultural power is never easy. At different times and in different places, however, it is more difficult or less. Today it is very difficult indeed—which explains why so few Christians or others are willing to do it. Many preachers, teachers, and ordinary folks go silent. Some even yield to ideologies that are antithetical to the moral teachings of Christianity and often the world's other major religious traditions and to the principles of natural law and natural rights that have shaped the best in our own cultural history, including the founding of the United States as a nation 'conceived in liberty and dedicated to the proposition that all men are created equal.' Albert Mohler, however, refuses to be bullied into acquiescence or silence. His is a prophetic and unapologetic Christian voice speaking truth to power. In every corner of the Christian community his words should be heard and heeded."

—ROBERT P. GEORGE, MCCORMICK PROFESSOR OF JURISPRUDENCE, PRINCETON UNIVERSITY

"In *The Gathering Storm*, Albert Mohler brilliantly addresses the primary worldview, cultural, and moral challenges of our day, showing us why these issues are so critical for us to comprehend. Recognizing that all too often Christians have struggled to grasp the far-reaching implications of these matters, this timely and theologically informed volume enables us to see with greater clarity the advances of secularization in all spheres of life. Moreover, Mohler, one of the twenty-first century's most incisive Christian thinkers, offers wise and insightful cultural commentary connected with an urgent warning about what is really at stake for individuals, families, churches, and the culture at-large. This excellent book should be essential reading for pastors, Christian educators, and laypersons across the land. Highly recommended!"

—DAVID S. DOCKERY, PRESIDENT, INTERNATIONAL ALLIANCE FOR CHRISTIAN EDUCATION; AND DISTINGUISHED PROFESSOR OF THEOLOGY, SOUTHWESTERN BAPTIST THEOLOGICAL SEMINARY

"Al Mohler's new book is for all people concerned about Western secularism's swelling tide, especially as it affects the church. His chapter on the church cites my own United Methodist denomination's civil war over marriage and sexuality, which should warn all Christians about compromising historic Christian ethical teaching. Heterodox theology and ethics are no longer just threats in liberal mainline denominations. They now swirl within evangelical churches. Mohler reminds us that these tides may swirl but they will not overwhelm the Rock."

—MARK TOOLEY, PRESIDENT OF THE INSTITUTE
ON RELIGION AND DEMOCRACY

THE GATHERING STORM

SECULARISM, CULTURE, AND THE CHURCH

R. ALBERT MOHLER JR.

NELSON
BOOKS

An Imprint of Thomas Nelson

Published in Nashville, Tennessee, by Nelson Books, an imprint of Thomas Nelson. Nelson Books and Thomas Nelson are registered trademarks of HarperCollins Christian Publishing, Inc.

Published in association with the literary agency of Wolgemuth & Associates, Inc.

Thomas Nelson titles may be purchased in bulk for educational, business, fund-raising, or sales promotional use. For information, please e-mail SpecialMarkets@ThomasNelson.com.

Unless otherwise noted, Scripture quotations are taken from the ESV® Bible (The Holy Bible, English Standard Version®). Copyright © 2001 by Crossway, a publishing ministry of Good News Publishers. Used by permission. All rights reserved.

Scripture quotations marked CEV are from the Contemporary English Version. Copyright © 1991, 1992, 1995 by American Bible Society. Used by permission.

Scripture quotations marked HCSB are from the Holman Christian Standard Bible®. Copyright © 1999, 2000, 2002, 2003, 2009 by Holman Bible Publishers. Used by permission. HCSB® is a federally registered trademark of Holman Bible Publishers.

Scripture quotations marked KJV are from the King James Version. Public domain.

Scripture quotations marked NIV are from the Holy Bible, New International Version®, NIV®. Copyright © 1973, 1978, 1984, 2011 by Biblica, Inc.® Used by permission of Zondervan. All rights reserved worldwide. www.Zondervan.com. The "NIV" and "New International Version" are trademarks registered in the United States Patent and Trademark Office by Biblica, Inc.®

Italics in Scripture have been added by the author for emphasis.

Any Internet addresses, phone numbers, or company or product information printed in this book are offered as a resource and are not intended in any way to be or to imply an endorsement by Thomas Nelson, nor does Thomas Nelson vouch for the existence, content, or services of these sites, phone numbers, companies, or products beyond the life of this book.

ISBN 978-1-4002-2023-6 (eBook)
ISBN 978-1-4002-2021-2 (HC)

Library of Congress Control Number: 2020933306

Printed in the United States of America
20 21 22 23 24   LSC   10 9 8 7 6 5 4 3 2 1

To Katie and Riley Barnes

Just a few years ago it was my honor to
introduce to the happy congregation
"Mr. and Mrs. Riley Barnes."
Our daughter and her husband united in marriage,
a new son a member of our family, faith, hope,
happiness, and love revealed again. Since then,
you have blessed us in countless ways, but Mary
and I count two gifts above all others.
Thank you for letting us share the unimaginable
joy of loving Benjamin and Henry as grandsons,
and for being such wonderful parents.
Your sweet home is filled with the love of
Christ and love for the church and constant
hospitality. Together, you are an oasis of joy.
We could not be more proud and thankful.

Love always, Papa

CONTENTS

INTRODUCTION

The Storm Gathers

Since I was in the eighth grade, Winston Churchill has been a figure of fascination and inspiration. One of the great leaders of history, he was also one of the most interesting personalities of any era. He lived his life on the stage of history, and he believed himself to be playing an important role on that stage. Indeed, the survival of freedom in the modern age cannot be told without him.

One great question has always vexed me. How could Winston Churchill's prophetic warnings about the rise of the Nazi threat have been so right, and yet so ignored, for so long? That is one of the great perplexities of the twentieth century.

For most of the 1930s, Churchill was a political outcast in Britain. Those were his "wilderness years," when Churchill was warning of the rise of Nazi Germany and the political class in Britain (and most of Europe) was determined not to see what Churchill saw. The horrors of the First World War were still too recent and too overpowering.

But Churchill was right, and that is why he was brought back into the government the very day that Britain declared war on Germany and finally moved to stop the march of Nazi aggression. That is why, in 1940, King George VI summoned Churchill to Buckingham Palace and asked him to serve as prime minister. The rest is history.

In his massive six-volume history of the war, Churchill entitled the first volume "The Gathering Storm," covering Europe's long years of denial about the Nazi threat. The title captured my attention years ago. Churchill's choice of words was perfect. He was documenting a storm that was gathering in public view for all to see—if they only *would* see. Summarizing his case, Churchill described the volume as the story of "how the English-speaking peoples through their unwisdom, carelessness, and good nature allowed the wicked to return."[1] And, of course, to rearm.

I have borrowed Winston Churchill's title, for I see a gathering storm that already presents itself as a tremendous challenge to the faithfulness of the Christian church. Actually, this storm has been on the horizon and working its way through history for over a century now, but in our own day with a dramatic strengthening and acceleration. This is the gathering storm of the secular age.

Historical analogies are always imperfect. The storm of the secular age is not so easily identified as the rise of the Nazi threat, nor is it focused on one movement, one leader, or even one readily summarized set of ideas. But, make no mistake, it is a storm.

My main point in borrowing Churchill's title is to borrow his main argument as well—the first task of faithfulness lies in understanding reality. Understanding the storm and seeing it for what it is turns out to be a necessary first step.

The increasingly secular character of our age presents Christians with a new and daunting set of challenges. We have witnessed the displacement of Christianity within the culture of the nations throughout Western Europe and Canada, and now in the United States as well. In the US, we can easily point to robust church attendance in some sectors and the more general fact that a majority of Americans still claim, in some sense, a Christian identity, but those numbers are falling fast.

In October 2019, the Pew Research Center released a major new report, "In U.S., Decline of Christianity Continues at Rapid Pace." The research indicates that though 65 percent of Americans identified as Christians when asked about their religion, that was actually a decrease of 12 percent in just ten years.[2] The math is easy to project into the future. The decline of Christian identity is particularly pronounced among younger Americans, and fully one-third of those age thirty-five and younger report no religious affiliation. Americans had long believed that we were an exceptional nation and that secularization was a European reality, not ours. We can afford that illusion no longer. America is on the same trajectory, just on a somewhat delayed timetable.

The most familiar word for the process we are witnessing is secularization. Scholars debate the term aggressively, but it points to a process that has been taking hold in modern societies since the dawn of the modern age. It does not mean that all people in these societies become truly secular, or irreligious, but it does mean that Christianity, which forged the moral and spiritual worldview of Western civilization, is being displaced. The society itself is progressively secularized.

The secular age is not inhabited by people who necessarily identify as secular. They may consider themselves "spiritual" and may even cite a religious affiliation as a matter of family identity. The key issue is that the society is distanced from Christian theism as the fundamental explanation of the world and as the moral structure of human society. Christian truth claims have lost all binding authority in the culture, and the loss of that binding authority is the most important fact. Most secular people claim no aggressively secular identity, but biblical Christianity no longer binds their consciences or grounds their fundamental values.

Oliver Roy, a prominent observer of secularization in the European context, correctly argues that the argument over secularization theory misses the essential point—that Western societies are being progressively "dechristianized." Sadly, as he noted: "Dechristianization never takes a step backward."[3]

Sometimes, the process is demanded by secularists, who see

belief in God as a great obstacle to human progress. For the most part the real challenge is not secularism, but secularization—a process that happens in a society largely without argument or notice. The binding authority of Christian theism—the biblically grounded understanding of God and the world—just fades away, replaced with a new worldview.

In his recent book, *Dominion: The Making of the Western Mind*, historian Tom Holland argued that our civilization cannot be understood without the central role played by Christianity. He went on to argue that even our secular age cannot be understood apart from the historic framework of Christianity. He documented the rise of major moral and political movements of modern times and made the case that they are extensions of Christian moral impulses, even if their basic ideology is secular. In an amazing sentence, he wrote: "Christianity, it seemed, had no need of actual Christians for its assumptions still to flourish."[4]

That sentence makes no sense to a believing Christian. It is simply untrue that Christian morality can exist for long without Christian belief. The residual influence of biblical Christianity in the larger culture existed for some time, but the pressures of the late modern age, and especially of the sexual revolution, are eroding and openly opposing even that residual influence.

Holland is right that our culture, even in its present secularizing form, cannot be explained without Christianity. But, by now, it is clear that those who are in the driver's seat in our culture are doing their best to deny that history and to marginalize the Christian worldview in the dominant society.

The secular age writes checks it cannot cash. It claims to uphold human rights even as it undercuts any argument for human dignity and natural rights. It invents new rights (like same-sex marriage) at the expense of fundamental rights (such as religious liberty). It claims a high view of human dignity, but aborts millions of unborn human beings in the womb. The pattern goes on and on.

A half century ago, the German intellectual Ernst-Wolfgang Böckenförde presented what is now known as the "Böckenförde Dilemma": "Does the free, secularized state exist on the basis of normative presuppositions that it itself cannot guarantee?"[5] That is a central dilemma of our times. Severed from the Christian worldview that gave it birth, the modern Western worldview cannot account for human dignity, human rights, or any objective system of right and wrong. As Quaker theologian D. Elton Trueblood warned many years ago, America and it allies were fast becoming "cut-flower civilizations," which, cut off from Christian roots, were destined to wither and die.[6]

There is now a robust debate among conservative theologians and political theorists over the question of the classical liberal tradition that became the framework for the concept of liberty that has been treasured by what Churchill called "the English-speaking world." This tradition became the central argument for the ordered liberty and constitutional self-government of the British and American political traditions. But classical liberalism (which produced both the conservative and the liberal political arguments in the United States) is now breaking down.

A central fact of the storm now gathering strength is moral liberalism, which cannot be explained without the dechristianization of society. Moral liberalism has basically become the dominant moral commitment of the most influential sectors of American society, from the universities to the entertainment industry and the artistic centers and the mass media and the titans of Silicon Valley. Apparently, to be hyper-modern is also to be hyper-liberal in moral worldview.

Do Christians believe enough biblical truth to withstand the moral liberalism of the age? Cultural forms of Christianity have been largely dechristianized and tamed, and nominal Christianity is fast disappearing. There is no social capital to be gained by joining a congregation defined by biblical truth. To the contrary, such membership will now destroy social capital. Liberal Protestantism is the quintessence of cultural Christianity, and the culture prevailed over Christianity long ago. Are evangelicals and other conservative Christians in the United States prepared to be considered enemies of the regime?

Political scientist Patrick J. Deneen understands that political and moral liberalism now lacks even the self-awareness to recognize the abyss. In his words, "The breakdown of family, community, and religious norms and institutions, especially among those benefiting least from liberalism's advance, has not led liberalism's discontents to seek a restoration of those norms. That would take effort and sacrifice in a culture that now diminishes the value of both."[7]

One of Winston Churchill's great virtues was his ability to see the storm and then to summon the courage and conviction to go into the storm. That is the challenge faced by Christians in the United States today—to see the storm and to understand it, and then to demonstrate the courage to face the storm. We must see the storm and understand it, if we are to be faithful to Christ in this secular age.

As Churchill observed as he brought that first volume of his great history of World War II to a close: "Facts are better than dreams."[8]

ONE

THE GATHERING STORM OVER WESTERN CIVILIZATION

It was as if Western civilization was burning, right before our eyes. The great cathedral known throughout the centuries as Notre-Dame de Paris burned through the April night, and the damage was catastrophic. The majestic cathedral that had symbolized Paris for more than nine hundred years was a smoldering ember.

Notre Dame's iconic image is more than a feat of architectural genius; the cathedral stood as an essential monolith of Western civilization, signifying the central role of Christianity in the development of European identity. Indeed, the very design of the structure itself marked the emergence of Gothic architecture—an architectural style intended above all else to communicate the transcendence and glory of God. Gothic architecture intends to make a person entering through its space feel small, almost *infinitesimal*. The seemingly endless perpendicular lines lead the eyes upward even as the magnitude of the space appears breathtaking. The message sent by the architecture of the cathedrals was clear—the cosmos is all about the glory of God.

The great cathedrals of Europe, and their successors elsewhere, were intended to make a huge statement of Christian identity for the entire society. For centuries, the landscape of Europe would be dominated by the cathedrals and their soaring towers and spires. The message would be clear.

The relevance of Notre Dame's fire to the crisis of Western civilization was there for all to see, but few seemed to see it. The story of Western civilization cannot be told without the cathedrals of Europe. The fact that cathedrals like Notre Dame would for centuries dominate the skyline of European cities points to the central role of Christianity in providing the worldview that made Western civilization possible. The basic tenets of Christian theology and ethics constructed the superstructure of European culture, providing its morality, basic truth claims, understanding of the cosmos, and language of meaning.

And all of that was burning, but the threat to the values of Western culture had already been burning for some time.

Notre Dame's history chronicles the erosion of Christianity's dominance over Western civilization. The gathering storm of secularism can be told through the narrative of arguably the most recognized cathedral in the world. More than mere bricks and mortar, Notre Dame's story captures the sorrow of secularism and its corrosive determination to exterminate the influence of the Christian worldview.

A Tale of the Times

When the French Revolution swept through the streets of Paris, the radical revolutionaries sought to eradicate the Christian heritage of France. On October 10, 1793, the revolutionaries marched into Notre Dame and replaced the statue of the Virgin Mary with a statue to the goddess of reason.

And so, a society framed, forged, and founded entirely upon the

Christian worldview tried to purge itself of all Christian vestiges. The French Revolution pursued a radical vision of a secular worldview governed not by religious belief, but by the Cult of Reason. But, predictably, the Cult of Reason failed—it could not maintain the revolutionary movement. When the French Revolution dethroned God, it plunged French society into "The Terror"—a mayhem of madness and murder. The revolution revealed secularism's utter inadequacy to establish a civilization and order a society.

Thus, in 1794, what was called the Cult of the Supreme Being replaced the Cult of Reason. This in no way marked a return by the French to the God of Abraham, Isaac, and Jacob—they did not return to the trinitarian God of the Bible. Instead, the French created a new god in their own image. They created a new cosmic deity they hoped would serve as a necessary check upon revolutionary passions.

Then, in 1801, Napoleon reestablished the Roman Catholic Church as the state religion in France, but he did so as a pointed maneuver. The church remained subservient to the autocratic and totalitarian regime of Napoleon Bonaparte as emperor. He did not grant the church autonomy in his empire; but he understood the church's value as an institution of morality, which he saw as necessary for a well-ordered society. Napoleon viewed the Christian tradition pragmatically—a tool to maintain order rather than the foundation of a societal worldview. Indeed, by the early twentieth century, the French government even claimed ownership of the major church buildings in France, including Notre Dame.

It is the French state, therefore, which is to rebuild Notre Dame, not the Roman Catholic Church. Though the Catholic Church utilizes the cathedral for its religious purposes, it does not own the cathedral. Furthermore, the French are now engaged in a great debate over the future of the cathedral. Will it be returned to its formal grandeur, or will it now become a monument to post-modern confusion? More likely, it will be the latter.

When the storm of secularism thunders on the horizon, it often seems unassuming, undaunting, a mere change in the weather. But secularism will seduce a civilization away from the very foundations that it stood upon for centuries. The tale of Notre Dame points to the endgame of secularism: what was once a testament to Christianity's centrality to the culture is now mostly a civic monument and symbol of French nationalism. Indeed, when the French president Emmanuel Macron issued his statement, he mourned the loss of a national treasure—a sentiment devoid of theological reflection or the significance of the cathedral within the nation's Christian heritage.

This is no longer a surprising response, and the pattern is hardly limited to France. Something fundamental has reshaped our entire culture. In Europe, the process is now very advanced, and the dechristianization of European societies is now largely true in Canada, where the society is in this respect far more like Europe than the United States, which is right across its border. In the US, we can see the same process now in play, and accelerating. Eventually, this process will reshape the entire culture. It is happening right now, right before our eyes.

The Secular Advance

The West's new cultural and moral environment did not emerge from a vacuum. Massive intellectual changes have shaped and reshaped Western culture since the dawn of the Enlightenment. At the heart of this great intellectual shift is a secular reframing of reality.

Secular, in terms of contemporary sociological and intellectual conversation, refers to the absence of any binding theistic authority or belief. It is both an ideology, which is known as *secularism*, and a consequence, which is known as *secularization*. The latter is not an ideology; it is a concept and a sociological process whereby societies become less theistic, and in our context that means less Christian in general outlook. As societies move into conditions of deeper and more progressive modernity, they move out of a situation in which religious belief—and specifically, belief in the God of the Bible—provided the binding authority that held society together and provided a common morality, a common understanding of the world, and a common concept of what it meant to be human. Secularizing societies move into conditions in which there is less and less theistic belief and authority until there is hardly even a memory that such a binding authority had ever existed.

The secularization of Europe has happened over the course of more than two hundred years. What began as a parlor game of the philosophers has now become the ideological engine of society. In Europe, events like the French Revolution were accelerants, but so were two devastating world wars in the twentieth century. For many reasons, America did not track with Europe's secularization schedule. For at least a century, America resisted the secularization of Western society in ways that perplexed many in the intellectual class. In some Scandinavian countries, less than 2 percent of the people attend church regularly, whereas an estimated 40 percent of Americans at least claim to be regular church attendees. The vast majority of Americans at least say they believe in God. Those statistics have led many American Christians to believe that the majority of Americans share the same general beliefs about God, morality, and the meaning of the world.

Yet, there is one sector of American public life that has kept pace with Europe's secularization—American universities. If secularization is ultimately about the evaporation of religious belief and its binding authority, then this process has certainly prevailed in the American university culture. The closer one gets to most American colleges or universities, the closer one gets to a secular public space—an intellectually secular place. Moreover, the engines of the culture are the intellectual elites. And where are they gathered in the most concentrated form for optimal influence upon the young? On the college and university campus. The intellectual class and the academic elites, representing a far more radical vision of America than what most of America understood, saw where the future lives—in the youth.

The secularization that America has largely avoided in the past is alive in its institutions of higher learning and has finally been unleashed on the nation through many successive generations of students who have had their worldview shaped by the secular, intellectual elites. Thus, the intellectual conditions of America are quantitatively and qualitatively different from those that prevailed in the culture just twenty years ago. The storm of secular thought, which has inundated the nations of Europe, has now spread over the Atlantic. We can now see the effects on our society, with a revolution in morality, ethics, and total worldview on the horizon.

The American and European thinkers who first tried to understand what was happening thought of religion's decline—Christianity specifically—as a process that the modern age would unleash automatically. To be modern would be to abandon belief in God. The old Christian morality would melt away and a new secular morality, including a new sexual morality, would replace it.

But, as it happened, the hard atheism and agnosticism that marked the intellectual and political elites was not followed by the general population. Instead, what happened among the millennials was the advance of a great religious indifference. In the words of Stephen Carter, a law professor at Yale University, God became a hobby, with fewer and fewer serious hobbyists.[1]

Peter Berger, one of the most insightful scholars of secularization, came to the conclusion that the United States was secularizing, but following a different pattern than was seen in Europe.[2] As Berger has explained, in twentieth-century America, Christianity and religion in general were transformed to something noncognitive and optional. Belief and doctrines became less important, and often receded in meaning. As a result, the binding authority of the Christian moral tradition or of any religious tradition was lost. Consequently, many of our friends and neighbors continue to profess faith in God, but that profession is increasingly empty of any moral authority or serious intellectual content. From the outside looking in, America did not appear to be secularizing at the same rate as Europe. In reality, however, professions of faith in God had less and less real theological or spiritual substance. America is slipping into its own Notre Dame moment—and our own society is far more secular than most Americans understand. And now, the leading trends in the United States point toward a far more aggressive secularization in the future. America is beginning to look like Europe, and it appears to be catching up fast.

Berger predicted that the collapse of conscious religious commitments coupled with the breakdown of binding authority would lead to the fact that, in the face of cultural opposition, belief in God or religious principles would quickly capitulate to the secular agenda—which is exactly what is happening in the larger culture. Just ten years ago, most polls showed that a majority of Americans opposed same-sex marriage. Yet, in our day, a majority—that includes many of the very same people polled one decade ago—has rendered an opposite moral judgment on the same issue. Just as Berger explained, when the cultural tide turned against our society's empty religious commitments, people were happy to jettison their moral judgment on homosexuality in order to retain their social standing. They adjusted their religious beliefs and moral judgments in order to be "on the right side of history," as the culture's progressives directed.

One of the clearer developments in the past two decades has been the inevitable collision between religious liberty—America's most cherished "first freedom"—and the newly invented sexual liberties. Most urgently, the collision was caused by the legalization of same-sex marriage by the Supreme Court in 2015. In recent years, it has become clear that the entire LGBTQ movement represents a clear challenge to anyone who would hold to the historic, biblical position on sexual morality and marriage.

Thus, the backdrop of the 2020 presidential election further reveals the pervasive secularism redefining the traditional foundations of Western civilization. The Democratic primary has especially highlighted the pace of secularism's demands. Many of the candidates ran as far to the left as possible, attempting to outdo one another in radical positions that would have been unthinkable in their party only four years ago. What political reality have we slipped in to where Senator Kirsten Gillibrand of New York and a former contender for the Democratic presidential nomination argued for the abortion of unborn babies as *the Christian* thing to do?

Indeed, the candidacy of South Bend mayor Pete Buttigieg—who is homosexual and married to a man—serves as a prime example. Buttigieg identifies as a Christian and a member of the Episcopal church, and he calls for a resurgence of liberal Christianity. In his view, the eclipse of traditional Christian sexual morality is a liberation of human sexuality. In effect, he claims a Christian identity while excavating Christianity of its nonnegotiable teachings, including the very definition of marriage. But there is no true Christianity without this truth and doctrine. Buttigieg is symbolic of secularizing Christianity that does not embrace a hard form of secularism. Buttigieg's candidacy shows the radical shift in the understanding of Christianity in our culture and its attempt to depart from the explicit teachings of the Bible—a departure of Christianity from its historic and scriptural roots. Buttigieg, moreover, contended that his Christian faith led him to no other conclusion than a secular, progressive agenda, which supports unfettered access to abortion and every aspect of the sexual revolution. Buttigieg tried to make a *theological* argument for rejecting historic Christian teaching. He asserted a new secular orthodoxy as the only viable way to read the

Bible. He posited a place for religion in the public square, but only a religion in line with his secularized theology.

Buttigieg's candidacy, though important as a political development, is even more important as an indicator of the direction in which our culture is headed. Historic Christianity is now increasingly either rejected outright or relegated to having no significance in the culture. Or, as in the case of Buttigieg, Christianity is redefined to meet the new "arc" of progressive morality.

The Impossibility of Belief

The Canadian philosopher Charles Taylor has carefully traced the influence and effects of secularization on the Western world. As he explained in his important book *A Secular Age*, the way people hold to theological convictions and religious principles in the modern era is fundamentally different from how people believed in the past.[3] Modernity has made religious belief provisional, optional, and far less urgent than it was in the premodern world. As Taylor noted, on this side of modernity, when people believe, they make *a choice to* believe that previous generations did not make. For many people, belief is now nothing more than an exercise of personal autonomy.

Taylor also helpfully showed that Western history can be defined by three intellectual epochs: pre-Enlightenment impossibility of unbelief; post-Enlightenment possibility of unbelief; and late-modern impossibility of belief. In the pre-Enlightenment era, it was impossible not to believe. One simply could not explain the world without some appeal either to the Bible or to some other form of supernaturalism. No other worldviews were available to members of society other than supernatural worldviews, particularly the Christian worldview in the West. While society had its heretics, there were no real atheists among them. Everyone believed in some form of theism, even if it was confused.

9

That all changed with the Enlightenment and the availability of alternative worldviews. These new alternative worldviews made it possible for members of society to reject the supernaturalism of Christianity or other theistic systems in exchange for a naturalistic worldview. At this point it became *possible not to believe.* Yet, even in this intellectual climate, it was still unlikely that the average educated person would reject the Christian worldview because the theistic explanations for life were simply more pervasive, binding, and persuasive than nontheistic worldviews.

But for many people in the present age, it is the third intellectual condition that prevails. In their mental and social world, it is *impossible to believe.* That means, especially in terms of the intellectual elites and the culture formative sectors of society, theism is not an available worldview. Many people in the most privileged sectors of our modern societies do not even *know* a believing Christian. They are no longer even haunted by the remains of a Christian frame of mind. They are truly secular.

Significantly, Taylor pinpoints this unbelief as a lack of conscious commitment to a self-existent, self-revealing God. Secularization is not about rejecting all religion. Taylor noted that people in the current hyper-secularized culture in America often consider themselves to be religious or spiritual. Secularization, according to Taylor, rejects belief in a personal God, one who holds and exerts authority. He described the secular age as deeply "cross-pressured" in its personal experience of some spirituality and rejection of the personal authority of God. The issue is binding authority.

In these cultural conditions, Christians are the new intellectual outlaws. Entering a discussion based on a theistic or theological claim is to break a cardinal rule of late modernity by moving from a proposition or question to an obligation; or moving from an "is" to an "ought." Some "oughts" remain, of course, but the language of command and law and authority have been explicitly secularized and carefully reduced in scope. Secularization in America has

HUMAN SELF-DEFINITION: WE ARE WHAT WE CHOOSE TO BE!

been attended by a moral revolution without precedent and without endgame. The cultural engines of progress driving toward personal autonomy and fulfillment will not stop until the human being is completely self-defining. This process requires the explicit rejection of Christian morality for the project of human liberation.

In 1983, theologian Carl F. H. Henry prophetically warned,

> If modern culture is to escape the oblivion that has engulfed the earlier civilizations of man, the recovery of the will of the self-revealed God in the realm of justice and law is crucially imperative. Return to pagan misconceptions of divinized rulers, or a divinized cosmos, or a quasi-Christian conception of natural law or natural justice will bring inevitable disillusionment. Not all pleas for transcendent authority will truly serve God or man. By aggrandizing law and human rights and welfare to their sovereignty, all manner of earthly leaders eagerly preempt the role of the divine and obscure the living God of scriptural revelation. The alternatives are clear: we return to the God of the Bible or we perish in the pit of lawlessness.[4]

Writing even earlier, Henry had already identified the single greatest intellectual obstacle to a cultural return to the God of the Bible. Released in 1976, Henry's first volume of his six-volume magnum opus *God, Revelation, and Authority* began with this line: "No fact of contemporary Western life is more evident than the growing distrust of final truth and its implacable questioning of any sure word."[5] This obstacle inhibiting the return to the authority of a Christian worldview is part of a vicious circle that begins with the departure from at least a cultural impression of God's revealed authority. Departing a Christian worldview leads to a distrust of final truth and a rejection of universal authority, which then hides the way back to the God of the Bible.

The story of the rise of secularism is a stunning intellectual and moral revolution. It defies exaggeration. We must recognize that it is far more pervasive than we might want to believe, for this intellectual revolution has changed the worldviews of even many of those who believe themselves to be opposed to it. If nothing else, many religious believers in modern societies now operate as theological and ideological consumers, constantly shopping for new intellectual clothing, even as they believe themselves to be traditional believers. They are the same old words, after all.

Christian ministers, theologians, and thinkers who stand on biblical authority break the rules by engaging the culture based on the self-revelation of a self-existent God with ultimate moral authority who has addressed his creatures with *oughts* and who does and will finally judge according to his laws and commands. This culture grows more and more resistant to a God—any god—who would speak to us with words such as "Thou shalt" and "Thou shalt not." The fact that Christians enter every conversation as believers in the Lord Jesus Christ who are bound by biblical revelation means they cannot begin without breaking the new rules. And we must remember those who break the rules are not welcome by those who *make* the rules.

We Must Protest

Christians reading this may respond in one of two ways. One, we can respond in utter despair, retreating together to the corners of coffee shops with a false sense of nostalgia that longs for the past—usually idealized. But, as biblical Christians, we are called to live in the present and prepare the next generation for the future.

The second response is equally erroneous. We might be tempted to look for rescue in political victory—believing that a retreat of secular thinking is only one election away. In other words, Christians might, and indeed have, attempt to rescue society through a social, political movement. While we must never demean the importance of elections nor diminish the responsible stewardship Christians have with their vote, we also dare not believe political victory will secure ultimate and lasting peace. Rescue will not come by mere politics. We do not need a political movement. We need a theological protest.

True Christianity and true gospel preaching depend on a firm commitment to the authority of Scripture. That is why, since the time of the Enlightenment, the inspiration, inerrancy, and authority of Scripture have been under constant attack. In the Enlightenment, modernist philosophers such as Descartes, Locke, and Kant confronted Western culture with a series of questions that ultimately transformed the notion of truth in the Western mind. The result was a totalitarian imposition of the critical model of rationality upon all truth, the claim that only scientific data can be objectively understood, objectively defined, and objectively defended. In other words, the modernist worldview does not allow for the concept of special revelation and openly attacked the possibility of supernatural intervention in world history. Modernity thus presented the church of the Lord Jesus Christ with a significant intellectual crisis.

In the United States, a quintessentially American philosophy known as pragmatism also challenged the ultimate authority and truthfulness of Scripture. Pragmatism was the idea that truth is a matter of social negotiation and that ideas are merely instrumental tools whose "truthfulness" will be determined by whether they meet the particular needs of the present time. In the eyes of the pragmatists, ideas are nothing but provisional response to actual challenges; and truth, by definition, is relative to the time, place, need, and person.

As most of us are aware, modernity has given way to post modernity, which is simply modernity in its latest guise— postmodernism is nothing more than the logical extension of modernism in a new mood. Claiming that all notions of truth are

= ULTRA MODERNISM
OR
HYPER MODERNISM

socially constructed, postmodernists are committed to total war on truth itself. This is the consequence of the secularization that has poisoned Western civilization. Secularization has birthed this postmodern moment, which has led to a deconstructionist project bent on the casting down of any religious or theological authority.

Christians must not retreat nor find our salvation in a false hope. We must, with every fiber of our God-given strength, with full dependence upon the power of the Holy Spirit, with every ounce of conviction we can muster through prayer, with unwavering courage, *protest* this secular moment.

The only way to escape the rationalist claims of modernism or the hermeneutical nihilism of postmodernism is the doctrine of revelation—a return to the doctrine of *sola Scriptura*. Christians must remember that in the doctrine of the inspiration and authority of Scripture bequeathed to us by the Reformers, we can have confidence in God's Word despite the philosophical and theological problems of the age. God has spoken to us in a reasonable way, in language we can understand, and has given us the gift of revelation, which is God's gracious disclosure of himself.

The gathering storm over Western civilization—the secularism that has wrought utter moral chaos in places like Europe—has blanketed the horizon in deep shadow and darkness. So many have celebrated this unforgiving storm. But Christians are in a unique predicament. We can confront the culture because we truly love our neighbor, and as such we work for the preservation of what is good and faithful—good laws that promote human dignity and uphold justice and righteousness. But, at the same time, we cannot attribute ultimate allegiance to any culture, but only to the Lord Jesus Christ.

Today's evangelicals, as the theological heirs of Martin Luther, John Calvin, and many others, cannot capitulate to the demands for a revolution in Christian doctrine and morality. An affirmation of the divine inspiration and authority of the Bible has stood at the center of the evangelical faith since the sixteenth century—and as the heirs of the Christian faith for more than two thousand years. We are those who confess, along with the faithful throughout the centuries, that *when Scripture speaks, God speaks.* Scripture alone is the ultimate authority for life and doctrine. In a sense, a Christian theology hangs on the accuracy of that singular proposition.

The Christian church cannot long survive without the church's explicit commitment to the authority of Scripture, and to the Lord Jesus Christ above all else. Without the authority of Scripture, our theological convictions will mirror the secularism of the larger society—we will merely espouse conjectures rather than finite and lasting convictions, and our preaching will dwindle to nothing more than a display of empty promises.

As Christians continue to face the stiff wind of opposition from the storm of the secular age, we must continue to be faithful. We must say and tell what we know to be true. We must protest every false gospel and every erroneous worldview that diminishes human flourishing. We must continue to hold fast to the core theological convictions of the Christian faith and to the primacy and authority of Scripture. We must not fail in seeing Scripture rightly proclaimed, the church built up, and the message of the gospel stretched to every corner of the earth.

All Authority

The secular age undermines the very conditions that make our civilization possible. The secular storm we face undercuts all notions of authority, placing on the throne the subjective self—a false notion of liberated humanity freed from the shackles of theism and the biblical worldview. The gathering storm we face threatens nothing less than a regime change—to inaugurate a new empire under the guise of human freedom and autonomy. Its consequences would be devastating. When society jettisons objective truth, it leaps down a rabbit hole even Alice of Wonderland would not dare to explore. It is fitting, therefore, to begin this book with the gathering storm over the entirety of Western civilization. Every subsequent chapter details an aspect of the coming crisis. The secular tide, much like the Nazi horde Churchill and the United Kingdom faced in the Battle for Britain, will eventually reshape every dimension of our society.

By now, just about every thinking person acknowledges that massive and powerful forces are reshaping our world and fundamentally altering our culture. But Christians never panic. We believe in the Lord Jesus Christ. We face the truth and see reality. We are concerned, aware, diligent, discerning, caring, and sometimes, even heartbroken. We see the gathering storm for what it is, and we dare not deny it.

Before Jesus left his disciples to build the church, he departed with these thunderous words: *"All authority* in heaven and on earth has been *given to me.* Go therefore and make disciples of all nations, baptizing them in the name of the Father and of the Son and of the Holy Spirit, teaching them to observe all that I have commanded you. And behold, I am with you always, to the end of the age" (Matt. 28:18–20).

Christians not only must confront this storm with the gospel of Jesus Christ, we must do so with full faith. Our hope does not rest with temporal political victory—though it understands the importance of politics—it rests in the One who sits at the right hand of the throne of God; it rests with the One through whom all things were created. Our faith is in the One who was nailed to the cross, rose from the grave, ascended into heaven, and established his unchallenged rule over the cosmos. Death is defeated, the head of the serpent crushed. The attempt of secularism to usurp the rule of the Son of God amounts to the height of human folly. *Nothing* will prevail over our God. *Nothing* can withstand the power of the gospel.

Christians, therefore, cannot be silent. We see the gathering storm and understand what it means—and what we are to do. We have a real and undeniable political responsibility. Indeed, we face issues like abortion and the dignity of human life. We bear a very real cultural responsibility. We may not produce the culture, but we operate in the culture and are stewards of the gospel in our cultural context. We have many responsibilities as Christians, but we have one gospel hope—the gospel of Jesus Christ. We must be, as the apostle Paul said, "not ashamed of the gospel, for it is the power of God for salvation to everyone who believes" (Rom. 1:16).

We are called to be faithful in the kingdom of this world, but our ultimate allegiance is to the kingdom of Christ—and to his kingdom alone.

TWO

THE GATHERING STORM IN THE CHURCH

By the end of the twentieth century, the impact of theological liberalism was seen in almost every denomination. The demands for an updated theology and morality—for Christianity to be redefined for a secular age—were reshaping seminaries, congregations, Christian schools, and denominations. Most of the old mainline denominations had capitulated by the 1970s. Tellingly, even as the prophets of theological liberalism had promised that liberalism would save their churches, it was actually liberal theology that led to the evacuation of those churches and denominations. Their membership and attendance plummeted. As recently as 2018, one liberal denomination in Canada predicted that by 2040 it would have "no members, no attendees, no givers."[1] No problem? This was even the truth in the Southern Baptist Convention until conservatives were able to redirect the denomination in the last years of the twentieth century.

As the present century dawned, secular trends in the society were well documented and a general religious decline marked many denominations of the culture. Conservative, biblically committed Christians faced a new set of challenges.

J. Gresham Machen, the great Presbyterian theologian from the early decades of the twentieth century, brilliantly assessed the state of modern Christianity and the rise of Protestant liberalism. Rather than seeing liberal theology as a variant of the Christian faith, Machen labeled it as a totally new religion that merely poses as Christianity. For Machen, nothing unified orthodox Christianity with Protestant liberalism—the former pursued theological fidelity to the God of the Bible, while the latter morphed into an entirely new religion. He titled his famous book *Christianity and Liberalism*, and made it clear that liberalism was an entirely new and separate religion altogether.

Liberal Protestantism and secularization have merged, creating a new and dangerous context for biblically committed Christians. This new context will reveal the true followers of Christ—and they may well be revealed by the fact that they are the last in our culture to remember what authentic Christianity is. The fusion of secularization with liberal Protestantism made liberal theology more normal in the eyes of the culture, for a secular culture does not even need a secular theology. They want no theology at all. But because of secularization's effect, liberal theology sometimes even infiltrates churches that think themselves to be committed to theological orthodoxy. Secularism has desensitized many people sitting in the pews of faithful, gospel-preaching churches, leading them to unwittingly hold even heretical doctrines. It is frightening to realize that some people can be so effectively secularized, even when regularly attending church. How? The fact is that many Christians will be hard-pressed to define faithful Christianity or to live and define central and eternal doctrines.

I have no doubt, for example, that many churches and their members would verbally assent to the reality and existence of an eternal hell; but this does not mean that they believe it consistently. The secular spirit—treating religion as a mere hobby—redefines essential Christian beliefs in subtle ways. Sociologist Christian Smith has described this reality as "Moralistic Therapeutic Deism," which is now believed by many who consider themselves faithful

Christians. Moralistic Therapeutic Deism consists of believing in some god who exists and created the world; a god who wants people to be simply congenial and kind; and that the goal of life is happiness and self-fulfillment. Perhaps most devastating is the general belief that good works secure a person's place in heaven.

The secular temptation confuses beliefs with emotions, suggesting that all that matters is feelings and fulfillment. As the society has become more secular, even faithful church members unwittingly adopt strange and unbiblical ways of thinking and believing. Furthermore, the ambient theological liberalism around us has made inroads into many churches. Secularization exerts upon the church both passive and active pressure. The pressure is passive in that as society turns away from any semblance of a biblical morality, churches sacrifice confessional conviction on the altar of cultural relevance. But the pressure is also active in that it often makes explicit demands on the church to surrender its essential theological claims. In the last century, the demand was to abandon doctrines such as the virgin birth and the bodily resurrection in order to be considered intellectually respectable. In our times, the pressure often takes the form of demands to abandon a biblical, sexual morality in order to be considered morally acceptable. That deal, by the way, never works, even socially. The secular demand is eventually for the abandonment of all doctrines and teachings that conflict with the Spirit of the Age. But where churches abandon these teachings, the larger society does not.

There is no external threat—even in a secular age—that can truly threaten the gospel of Christ, nor the eternal promises that Christ has made to his church. Indeed, Jesus' promise to his disciples in Matthew 16:18 is this: "On this rock I will build my church, and the gates of hell shall not prevail against it." Not even death will truly threaten the promises of God in the gospel of Christ. The great threat we face is not to the church's existence, but to its *faithfulness*. Nothing in the cosmos, not even the gale and torrent of a secular tide will negate the promise of Christ for his church. But the church's faithfulness is always at stake, and that is particularly true in a secular age. We must be aware, discerning, and careful in our thinking, our preaching, and how we raise our children. If people can be secularized within our churches, they can also be secularized while living in our homes—if we are not marked by conviction and faithfulness.

Passive Secularism

If we observe carefully, we can see how passive secularism infiltrates churches, inadvertently exerting a liberalizing pressure on Christians and denominations. Passive secularization works in subtle ways, applying pressure and influence rather than making overt demands. Passive secularization happens just because we are breathing the culture and constantly bombarded with cultural messages. Hollywood, the news media, and the culture-shaping forces of the society constantly tell us that right-minded and culturally acceptable people believe this and not that. The expectations of the culture shift and drag everything (and almost everyone) along.

Similarly, the secular age exerts a subtle but constant influence on churches and Christians. If not careful, churches will look less and less like churches and more and more like the secular world around them. In a sense, liberal theology begins to slowly replace orthodox faith. Or, in other cases, churches simply stop talking about or teaching important truths revealed in the Bible. The demand is to just be quiet. This is what happened to the doctrine of hell, which is clearly revealed in the Bible. As history revealed, hell just disappeared from the preaching of many churches, and no one seemed to notice. The same is true when it comes to many biblical teachings, ranging from divorse to the exclusivity of the gospel. In this respect, silence is decidedly *not* golden. The failure to teach truth eventually leads to failure of Christ's people even to *know* the truth.

Atheism: The New Orthodoxy

The United Church of Canada has recently dealt with an apparently confounding and controversial question: Can an atheist serve as a pastor? The pastor in question was Gretta Vosper, an avowed atheist who, in 2008, wrote the book *With or Without God*, which trivialized belief in God and replaced faith with her own concept of morality and virtue as the primary marks of a Christian. In 2013, Vosper made her atheism public, followed by a 2015 letter that she wrote in which she disparaged God's presence in the world and his activity in historical events. God could not be responsible, she argued, because God does not exist. Her argument: There is no God; no one's in charge. Accidents just happen. Belief in God, according to Vosper, belongs to an outdated worldview.

Interestingly, in her zeal to depart from an antiquated, theocentric worldview, Vosper's congregation *dramatically* shrunk in size. When she discarded the Lord's Prayer, her church deteriorated from 150 attendees to 50—an exodus of two-thirds of the congregation. It turns out that "cultural relevance," rather than saving a marginalized church, only hemorrhages to a swift demise.

Her atheism provoked the local jurisdiction of the United Church of Canada to conduct what Vosper labeled as a heresy trial. The local panel ruled her unsuitable for ministry and almost defrocked the atheist minister. Then, the national denomination conducted its final review of her case and subsequently reached a settlement with Vosper. The United Church of Canada explained its decision to end the investigation, stating, "This doesn't alter in any way the belief of the United Church of Canada in God."[2] In other words, atheism and theism are *not* incompatible in the view of this denomination. The requirement that one believe in God does not contradict the reality that one denies the existence of God. This is capitulation of the highest order. The United Church of Canada, by legitimizing atheism as a possible expression for its ministers, has actually erased all the lines, safeguards, and convictions that must guide the church of the Lord Jesus Christ. Nothing is out of bounds; nothing can cross the line because the line has disappeared. The United Church of Canada reduced belief in God to an outdated, outmoded, and inconsequential tenet of the Christian faith. It has become a parable—even a cartoon—of what happens when a church abandons the gospel. Now, even atheists can be ministers. Why not?

Julian Falconer, Vosper's attorney, explained why the United Church of Canada chose to settle rather than conduct a trial: "Both parties took a long look at the cost benefit at running a heresy trial, and whether it was good for anyone, and the results speak for themselves."[3] This explanation reveals an extremely important and harrowing reality and points to the devastation of secular ideology on a church. The United Church of Canada conducted a cost benefit analysis and decided that heresy was the lesser of two evils. The denomination weighed faith in God against "inclusivity" and valued inclusivism higher than theological fidelity. For the sake of the church, belief in God had to go.

Kevin Flatt's book *After Evangelicalism: The Sixties and the United Church* chronicles the theological downgrade of the United Church of Canada since the 1960s. Social justice concerns propelled the denomination rather than theological commitments. As such, this church became a servant to secularism and liberalism in Canada. It pioneered transgender ministers, supported abortion, and championed same-sex marriage, even before it became legal in Canada. Flatt's analysis identified the "keep up or die" trope that drove the denomination's theological deterioration.

The United Church of Canada is hardly alone in this. So many denominations are driven by this same secular impulse. They have surrendered theological conviction for the misguided hope that survival in this secular age hinges on abandoning the doctrines and truths of the gospel that have guided the church since its inception. The results of this idea, however, have devastated liberal churches. It turns out that "keep up *or* die" really means "keep up *and* die."

Losing the Church

In 2015, the United States Supreme Court issued a decision that legalized same-sex marriage across all fifty states. In its wake, there are clearly moments where the new sexual orthodoxy issues uncompromising demands upon what it defines as deviant worldviews, especially the biblical worldview. Yet, the legalization of same-sex marriage has also had an impact on churches and denominations trying to navigate these strange, new waters. What we find is similar to the secularization of the United Church of Canada—where one denomination now accepts the validity of an atheist pastor with other churches sending confusing signals on the clear, biblical teachings regarding marriage, gender, and sexuality.

While the issue of the LGBTQ revolution will be covered in a later chapter, it is important to see how secularization of the culture has led churches down a path toward a complete denial of the Scriptures, surrendering the glory of biblical marriage in order to remain culturally relevant and merely nice.

Just last year, an exchange took place between two Hollywood actors on the very question of gay marriage and the church. Ellen Page called out Chris Pratt in a tweet, stating, "If you are a famous actor and you belong to an organization that hates a certain group of people, don't be surprised if someone simply wonders why it's not addressed. Being anti LGBTQ is wrong. There aren't two sides. The damage it caused is severe. Full stop. Sending love to all." In the tweet, Page specifically indicted Pratt for his membership in what was alleged to be an anti-LGBTQ church. The church in question is Zoe Church, a church in association with the Hillsong movement. There can be no question that Page not only targeted Pratt but took direct aim at any organization or church that holds to anything even remotely connected to a biblically informed sexual ethic.

While Page's tweet represents active secularization—the explicit demands of a secular culture for Christians to surrender their theological commitments—Pratt's response highlights the reality of passive secularization. He stated,

> It has recently been suggested that I belong to a church which hates a certain group of people and is infamously anti LGBTQ. Nothing could be further from the truth. I go to a church that opens their doors to absolutely everyone. Despite what the Bible says about my divorce, my church community was there for me every step of the way, never judging, just gracefully accompanying me on my walk. They helped me tremendously, offering their love and support. It is what I have seen them do for others on countless occasions, regardless of sexual orientation, race, or gender. My faith is important to me, but no church defines me or my life, and I'm not a spokesman for any church or any group of people. My values define who I am. We need less hate in this world, not more. I am a man who believes that everyone is entitled to love who they want free from the judgment of their fellow man.

That last line encapsulates the modern secular orthodoxy—"Everyone is entitled to love who they want free from the judgment of their fellow man."

Pratt's response reveals at least two consequences of seductive secularization. First, pressure led Pratt to try and hold both a Christian commitment (of some sort) in one hand while simultaneously holding in his other hand a congeniality with the sexual revolution. To be clear, these are mutually exclusive worldviews, but such is the consequence of seductive secularization, which attempts to marry incompatible worldviews. In 2017, Carl Lentz, who serves as a pastor of the New York–based Hillsong church, missed several opportunities to clearly express a biblical view of homosexuality and same-sex marriage. In an interview with CNN, he gave a non-answer, stating, "It's not our place to tell anyone how they should live. That's their journey." Pratt's defense and

Lentz's dodge amount to nothing less than an abdication of biblical Christianity.

But both Pratt and Lentz reveal a further danger of passive secularization upon the church, namely, a diminishing ecclesiology. Where is Christ's church? What is a church? A true church does not give a non-answer to a direct biblical question. Pratt and Lentz represent the thinnest ecclesiology—a conception of the church severed from the Scriptures. Pratt claimed that "no church defines me or my life." According to the Bible, however, the church *does* define us. Whereas Pratt denies that his church defines him, the Scriptures teach that the church founded by Christ is the family of the living God, bought by the blood of Christ, in covenant together for the cause of the gospel. That is the vision of a biblical church. Such a church, bound together in obedience to Christ, absolutely defines a member's life. Moreover, Lentz's ambiguity in his 2017 CNN interview undermines the clear and glorious identity of the church of Jesus Christ. Lentz described the church as a body with no authority, nor responsibility to summon its members to Christian discipleship. Jesus commissioned his disciples to establish a church of obedient followers—sons and daughters of God who would devote their lives to the glory of Christ and his kingdom.

The passive pressures of secularization, therefore, inevitably undermine the ecclesial structures established by Christ in the New Testament. As the culture continues to secularize, and many churches surrender their authority as embassies of the gospel and succumb to the idolization of the self, individual autonomy usurps any objective, pervasive standard of conduct. Furthermore, the Great Commission is about making *disciples* who obey Christ's commands: "Go therefore and make disciples of all nations, . . . *teaching* them to *observe all* that I have *commanded* you" (Matt. 28:19–20, emphasis added).

Discipleship to Christ makes objective demands on conduct, virtue, and morality. The God revealed in holy Scripture issues commands to his people, and God calls his children to live in obedience to his commands and statutes. Indeed, as the apostle John wrote, "For this is the love of God, that we keep his commandments" (1 John 5:3). Where you find a church, you find a community of believers striving for holy obedience to God. Conversely, a church that doesn't tell people how to live in obedience to Christ isn't a church at all.

When so-called churches blur the lines on the authority of Scripture and surrender core theological commitments, they are slowly but surely giving way to the pressures of modernity. Indeed, the idolization of cultural relevance leads to theological confusion—a deliberately marked confusion.

At minimum, passive secularization contorts the hearts and minds of even those who claim to be faithful followers of Jesus Christ. We do not really believe the audacious, scandalous claims the Scriptures make, nor do we order our lives around the radical commands of Christ. In a secular age, everything appears to be negotiable. Doctrine can be reformulated. Anything objectionable to the *zeitgeist* can be removed. In a secularizing epoch, the church must constantly be aware of how even *our* thinking is seductively rearranged and recast. The only resistance comes by the faithful preaching of the Word of God—what the Reformers call the "ordinary means of grace." Where there is no consistent biblical preaching and teaching, expect theological chaos—and worse.

Active Secularization

While passive secularization presents a very real and pressing threat to the church, active secularization directly confronts the authority of the church and explicitly demands theological capitulation. The secular elites have a singular devotion toward the unconditional surrender of divergent, theistic worldviews—especially the Christian worldview.

Indeed, the hostility of secularism against the Christian world-view surfaced in an article from the *Guardian* with the headline "If We Reject Gender Discrimination in Every Other Arena, Why Do We Accept It in Religion?" Beatrice Alba, the author of the article, chillingly argued that parents, regardless of their religious beliefs, do not have the right to teach those beliefs to their children if those beliefs are hostile to the LGBTQ agenda. According to Alba, society has now progressed to the point where religious organizations, churches, and even individual Christians should no longer enjoy religious freedom—either they must surrender to the moral, secular revolution or they must go. Her article represents the full broadside of secularism against theism—a secular society will not tolerate any individual, institution, church, or denomination until it fully surrenders to a secular worldview. This is the demand of secularization upon the Christian community.

The active assaults of secularization on Christianity target not only specific theological claims but also the expressions of that theology in the public sphere. For example, consider the number of states and municipalities defunding or prohibiting Christian-based adoption and foster care agencies. Many of these agencies refuse to place children with same-sex couples due to the very clear religious beliefs that marriage is between one man and one woman. The secular revolutionaries, however, believe that these policies take the form of harmful, discriminatory prejudice—a prejudice that must cease.

Indeed, just last year, the Trump administration offered protection to religious adoption agencies besieged by the moral and sexual revolution. The revolutionaries forcefully demanded that these agencies either alter their policy or close their doors. Swift retribution came from Senator Ron Wyden of Oregon who said, "To turn away qualified parents because of their religion, sexual orientation, or gender identity and deny these kids a secure home is immoral."[4] To be clear, same-sex couples have other options to pursue adoption. The issue here isn't one of access but indignation toward the

Christian worldview. The message sent to Christian ministries is clear—go ahead and provide or fund social welfare agencies, but you must abandon your Christian convictions if you want to stay in business.

Sometimes, the assaults of secularization against Christianity jump right off the page or scream from the headlines. In 2018, an article appeared in *USA Today* by Baptist minister and lawyer Oliver Thomas with the headline "American churches must reject literalism and admit we got it wrong on gay people."[5] The article begins with a provocative statement: "Churches will continue hemorrhaging members until we face the truth: Being a faithful Christian does not mean accepting everything the Bible teaches." Specifically, Thomas targets the teachings of the Bible pertaining to sexual ethics and passages that expressly condemn homosexuality.

According to Thomas, the source of the church's error is not a misinterpretation of the Scriptures; rather, the Bible got it wrong—the biblical authors were bound by time, culture, and an antiquated worldview that wrongly defined and condemned homosexual behavior. Indeed, Thomas believes that the modern troubles plaguing the church stem from its erroneous approach to the Scriptures. He wrote, "Here is the corner we have painted ourselves into. *The Bible says it. I believe it. That settles it.* Yet, the Hebrew and Christian Scriptures did not float down from heaven perfect and without error. They were written by men, and those men made mistakes." In just a few words, Thomas denied the position of the believing church since its inception—that the Scriptures are holy and stand as the inspired, authoritative Word of the living God. This is an explicit denial of *sola Scriptura*. Indeed, it is certainly a denial of Scripture as Scripture.

The impetus of Thomas's charge is moral. The Bible does not correspond to his moral and ethical worldview, which celebrates the entire array of the LGBTQ spectrum. The sexual revolution has no compatibility with the Bible—so the Scriptures must be tossed out as erroneous (and dangerous) artifacts of a bygone age. This amounts to a complete, merciless assault against the authority of the Bible. Truth must now be defined by subjective emotivism rather than the enduring and objective truth from the transcendent God.

These active assaults against the Christian worldview have also abounded in the 2020 presidential election, perhaps most evidently with the candidacy of Pete Buttigieg, who has used his faith as a lightning rod for his campaign. Not since Jimmy Carter and Bill Clinton have we seen a Democratic candidate discuss his or her faith as explicitly as Pete Buttigieg—but his religious assertions mark a complete and total departure from the biblical worldview. Indeed, in a speech last year, Buttigieg took direct aim at Vice President Mike Pence, stating, "I wish that the Mike Pences of the world would understand . . . that if you have a problem with who I am, your problem is not with me. Your quarrel, sir, is with my creator."[6] The issue here is Buttigieg's homosexuality and his marriage to another man.

While Buttigieg acknowledges the existence of a Creator, he avows that his sexual identity exists as an extension of the Creator's will—God made him that way. This is a common argument from LGBTQ activists that now rings even louder with the candidacy of Buttigieg. The argument, however, in no way squares with biblical orthodoxy or the teachings of Scripture. Yet, Buttigieg demands that evangelical Christians "evolve" in their understanding of holy Scripture. The biblically orthodox interpretation of sexuality represents an antiquated morality from a culturally dated book. In Buttigieg's view, we ought to keep the universal principles but jettison the culturally and socially inconvenient passages that do not comport with our modern, moral ideology. Christians must, in short, redefine biblical sexuality in unbiblical terms.

Buttigieg's argument presses Christians to see homosexuality and LGBTQ identity as a gift from the Creator. Failure to evolve and to adopt an understanding of the Bible freed from the pre-modern worldview puts Christians on the wrong side of history. Now enters the cultural pressure directed against biblical Christians. The demand made by Buttigieg amounts to nothing less than coercive capitulation—a capitulation on deep issues of eternal significance. His candidacy demands that evangelical Christians see the light of progressive reasoning and reject the antiquated dogma of a bygone era. *If,* and *only if,* evangelicals capitulate on issues like marriage, gender, sexuality, and abortion will we have a seat at the table of public and political discourse.

The active assaults against biblical and orthodox Christianity descend from not only outside the church but inside its own walls. Last year, many around the world anticipated the results of the special General Conference of the United Methodist Church (UMC), which convened to discuss the doctrinal position of the UMC regarding homosexuality. For many decades the UMC trended toward Protestant liberalism—it was another tale of secularization providing the fuel for liberal theology to germinate and grow. Many believed the special session would end with yet another mainline denomination capitulating to the cultural whims and forces of secularization; how wrong they were.

After much maneuvering, the UMC turned back the effort to abandon its historic affirmation of biblical sexuality and marriage. The event was an earthquake of sorts, sending shockwaves around the world. The General Conference sustained its biblical standards on marriage as an exclusive union between one man and one woman and rejected the LGBTQ revolution. It was unprecedented. It was church history happening before our eyes—never has a mainline Protestant denomination long characterized by theological liberalism defeated the LGBTQ juggernaut and affirmed the biblical vision for marriage and sexuality.

As the sexual revolution targeted and captured many mainline Protestant denominations, the UMC special meeting held its ground. The committed conservatives within the church did not leave; they pressed on with convictional leadership as they attempted to stem the tides of secularism and liberal theology.

Nevertheless the active pressures of secularism pressed in on the UMC. This time, the pressure came from *within* the church. Adam Hamilton, the pastor of the largest UMC in the United States, suggested that all the texts in the Bible, including texts about human sexuality, must be sorted into three different buckets. The first bucket contains verses that never amounted to "the expression of God's will." The second bucket encompasses texts that, at one time, denoted the expressed will of God, but no longer. The last bucket holds texts that "are true expressions of God's will and always will be."

Hamilton has repeatedly denied the inerrancy of the Word of God. But he went even further and argued that human beings are to decide which biblical texts are—or ever have been—God's Word. The audacity of applying human reason to jettison verses as never expressing the will of God is arrogance of the highest order. Furthermore, some elite squad of hermeneutical hitmen are now to decide which verses go in which bucket. You can guess which texts get thrown into the first bucket quickly. Confusion begets confusion. Capitulation on first things sows capitulation over all things. When a church jettisons the fundamental doctrines of the faith, it will allow for any cultural anomaly to enter through its doors, all in the name of relevance.

The most urgent realization following the Methodist struggle was the fact that those pressing for liberalization *never gave up*. Even after the special General Conference defended the church's historic definition of marriage as the union of a man and a woman, and even after the church reaffirmed its commitment to biblical sexual morality, liberal bishops continued to undermine church authority, citing the higher authority of the LGBTQ revolution. Within months of the special meeting, it appeared that the church would eventually divide, with schism threatened. For those who dare defend biblical orthodoxy, there are no final victories—at least in this age.

On This Rock

The passive and active secularism and secularization threatens Christian fidelity. The secularization of the culture challenges the church and demands unconditional surrender. Within the walls of the church, we see continued efforts to undermine the authority of the Bible and usurp the rule of Christ, summoning the people of God to abandon their posts, and to redefine the Christian faith into something more "acceptable" in the view of the dominate culture. The church of Jesus Christ, however, must always live as a people of the Book—as scriptural people devoted to zealous study of God's Word. The Bible is the norming norm that cannot be normed. Christians must affirm biblical authority and always remember that when you surrender the authority of Scripture, you threaten the very existence of the church. Where you find a church, you find a community committed to the Bible. If not, you have not found a church.

Why must Christians hold fast to biblical authority at all costs? Because of something that happened in Matthew 16:13–18:

> Now when Jesus came into the district of Caesarea Philippi, he asked his disciples, "Who do people say that the Son of Man is?" And they said, "Some say John the Baptist, others say Elijah, and others Jeremiah or one of the prophets." He said to them, "But who do you say that I am?" Simon Peter replied, "You are the Christ, the Son of the living God." And Jesus answered him, "Blessed are you, Simon Bar-Jonah! For flesh and blood has not revealed this to you, but my Father who is in heaven. And I tell you, you are Peter, and on this rock I will build my church, and the gates of hell shall not prevail against it."

When Peter confessed that Jesus was the Christ, he made an acknowledgment unlike any other in the history of mankind. People around the world from every nation confer authority on their kings, queens, and democratic leaders. Even in the United States, we show honor and respect to our elected officials because of the office they hold. Citizens of every nation owe their allegiance to the authorities over them. But when Peter declared that Jesus was the Christ, the Son of the living God, he proclaimed the unassailable and universal rule of the one, true King over the cosmos. All other claims to authority, all other citizenry commitments to corporeal kingdoms pale beside the oaths Christians take to Jesus Christ, the Messiah, the Son of the living God.

Jesus affirmed Peter for his answer, but he also made clear that the truth that Jesus is the Christ, the Son of the living God, is a revealed truth—not a human discovery. Christ also declared that upon Peter's confession, he would build his church. This is essential for Christians living in this secular age, facing the secular storm. When churches and denominations surrender to the forces of secularism, they do so because they departed from the "rock," namely, the lordship of Jesus Christ. Jesus told his disciples that the confessional affirmation of his lordship is the immovable foundation upon which the church will stand. Jesus promised that nothing on earth, not even the gates of hell, will defeat Christ's church so long as it stands upon the rock of Christ and his lordship.

The lordship of Christ also demands that the church *live* out conviction and obey Christ in all his commands. The moral authority of the church has been seriously buffeted by the scandal of sexual immorality that is tolerated and the scandal of sexual abuse that has been denied. The obedient church of Jesus Christ cannot just preach a biblical morality; it must live out that morality. Otherwise, our words will ring hollow.

In the end, churches must stand for the faith once for all delivered to the saints. This means that our faith and theology extend from Christ and his apostles. We stand in that faith that Christ taught his church and continues to teach through the holy Scriptures. This is the faith that the true church has believed, confessed, and taught from the time of the New Testament until today.

Furthermore, churches must stand on preaching the Word of God as the first mark of the church. Where the Word of God is not rightly preached, there is no church. It's just that simple.

The church must also stand on confessional fidelity as a hallmark of its identity. The faith once delivered to the saints must be expressed and defined and defended in confessional form. The necessity of creeds and confessions is learned anew, often painfully, by every generation of Christians. We must define what we believe and hold each other accountable to that confessional identity. Churches and denominations that have no confession of faith, or have a confession in name only, disarm themselves doctrinally.

Churches must also stand for the totality of the Christian worldview. The Bible presents the only comprehensive, truthful, and universal view of the world. From Genesis to Revelation, the Bible offers Christians a pure theology that informed and instructed the church throughout every age. From the first centuries of the church's existence, to our own secular moment, the Bible consistently remains the safe haven for Christians to turn to as the source of their worldview.

Finally, churches must recommit to the Great Commision. This is the mandate to make Christ known to the nations. To know Christ is to obey his commandments, and this means taking the gospel to the ends of the earth. Christ alone reminds us of the truth that the gospel is the only saving message, and it is our responsibility to preach the gospel to the nations. This is our offensive strategy as the church—we do not hide behind our walls; we take the gospel to all the people of the world, even the secularized world. That is our calling.

Secularism's storm gathers over the church. It demands surrender and will not yield until the Christians capitulate to its challenge. For the church of Jesus Christ, we can endure this deluge. We can withstand the torrent of secularism. We can hold fast because we stand upon the rock—the immovable confession that Jesus Christ is Lord, the Son of God, the one who conquered the grave and promised that nothing will prevail against his church.

THREE

THE GATHERING STORM OVER HUMAN LIFE

Abortion looms as a great moral scar on the modern age—a singular symbol of the embrace of the culture of death in the most technologically advanced nations on earth. The scar runs openly through the American landscape. In one sense, Americans have been deeply divided over abortion for the last half century since the US Supreme Court's infamous *Roe v. Wade* decision of 1973. But, unlike the case in many other nations, and unlike the more liberal consensus that had delayed in the US on so many other issues, the debate over abortion in America is still fervent and it continues to shape American parties—all the way to the presidency.

As the late columnist Charles Krauthammer noted: "Of all the major social issues, abortion is the only one that has not moved towards increasing liberalization."[1] That observation is accurate. Though Americans have become more liberal on many issues (especially LGBTQ issues), the national conscience is still deeply divided over abortion, and five decades of abortion rights activism has not produced a liberal consensus. That is good news. But the bad news is that it matters a very great deal whether the unborn child lives in a womb in New York or in Alabama.

The horror of abortion seems to appear daily and in ever deadlier form in the nation's headlines as states across the country pledge their support for late-term abortion laws. These laws would essentially allow for abortion right up until the moment a child is born. Recently passed laws in New York and Rhode Island represent a new day in the pro-abortion movement, which endeavors to make the womb the most unsafe place for any baby in the United States. The totality of the English language fails to describe the utterly chilling and abhorrent barbarity of the pro-abortion movement's agenda.

In the past, pro-choice advocates have typically not openly defended abortion rights during the third trimester. Nevertheless, the truth was revealed when the pro-abortion movement vociferously opposed even a ban on partial-birth abortion. Most Americans—even most who say they favor some form of abortion rights—maintained that if a baby could survive outside the mother's womb, protection should be granted.

That has changed. The inevitable outcome of the pro-abortion worldview leads to abortion on demand at any moment of the pregnancy. States should, according to this radical dogma, protect a woman's right to abort at any time for any reason related to her health—health being defined not only as life and death, but emotional and mental. The deadly logic of the pro-abortion movement took an even deadlier turn on the American political scene over the last year—especially with the backdrop of the 2020 presidential election.

The pro-abortion movement has sown a culture of death. It attempts to destroy and to deny the sanctity of life, and the consequences are now clear to see. This is what happens when a society jettisons the moral code based in the truth that every human is an extension of God's common grace, and a bearer of God's image. Unless this march to death is reversed, the headlines will only become more horrifying and even deadlier.

Indeed, in 2018, the United States Senate attempted to reverse this pervasive culture of death through a resolution banning infanticide—legally defined as the taking of a living child. The move, however, failed to muster enough votes to protect the lives of children born *alive* after an attempted abortion. This vote comes as one of the most important events in recent American political history—and it is simultaneously tragic and telling. This latest failure to protect human life represents the latest chapter in America's lamentable and horrific culture of death—a culture primarily driven by the pro-abortion movement.

The Senate blocked a resolution that would punish any doctor who failed to provide medical care to a child born after an attempted abortion. A slim majority voted in favor of the legislation while forty-four senators voted against it. The number forty-four demands attention—forty-four United States senators voted *against* a bill banning infanticide. This is a chilling moment in American history.

Nebraska senator Ben Sasse, the author and main sponsor of the legislation, said, "I want to ask each and every one of my colleagues whether or not we're okay with infanticide. It is too blunt for many people in this body, but frankly, that is what we're talking about here today. . . . Are we a country that protects babies that are alive, born outside the womb after having survived a botched abortion?" Sasse described the legislation as an "infanticide ban" that would have protected the lives of innocent newborns who survived an abortion that failed.

The failure of this legislation shows the bare teeth of the pro-abortion movement and the death grip it holds upon the modern Democratic Party. The pro-abortion forces now push for radical abortion laws, which allow for abortions up to and even after a baby's due date. They advocate for abortions in every legal circumstance. The Christian worldview affirms the sanctity of human life at every moment, from fertilization to natural death. Thus every abortion amounts to the murder of an unborn child. Yet to this point, even the most radical pro-abortion lobbyists have shied away from public and eager support for late-term abortion. Now, however, all limits are off. There is no line too far and no moral absolute governs the pro-abortion ideology. Their only absolute is absolute support for abortion.

Only three Democrats dared to cross the aisle in support of this bill against infanticide. That fact is not surprising given the states those senators represent: West Virginia, Pennsylvania, and Alabama. Tellingly, all the contenders for the Democratic nomination for president serving in the Senate fell over themselves to record their opposition to this bill banning infanticide. This is the new moral vector of the Democratic Party heading into a presidential election cycle. This is now the party unwilling to protect the lives of babies born alive.

On the floor of the Senate, majority leader Mitch McConnell called the proposed law "a straightforward piece of legislation to protect newborn babies." He also indicted Democrats, arguing that they "seem to be suggesting that newborn babies' right to life may be contingent on the circumstances surrounding their birth." Senator McConnell rightly assessed the harrowing implications of the Democratic argument, but recently, the pro-abortion movement and its allies in Congress have continued to subvert the dignity of life from the moral compass of the American society—their party's majority even opposed the Partial-Birth Abortion Ban Act, which prevented and outlawed the most macabre murder of an unborn baby in the womb.

The measures promoted by the Democratic Party and the leftward lunge of the Democratic candidates to support the most radical abortion bills reveal the rise of the menacing culture of death. Indeed, the Democratic Party is beholden to the moral agenda of the Planned Parenthood Federation of America, the pro-abortion organization bent on securing unfettered and taxpayer-funded access to abortions for every woman no matter the circumstance, reason, or age of the child in the womb. Leana Wen, former president of the Planned Parenthood Federation of America, said, "We must call out today's vote for what it is: a direct attack on women's health and rights. This legislation is based on lies and a misinformation campaign, aimed at shaming women and criminalizing doctors for a practice that doesn't exist in medicine or reality."[2]

This is where the arguments from the pro-abortion agenda break down and depart from any intellectual honesty or consistency. First, they argue that the practice does not exist. But if the practice does not exist, why oppose a bill that would outlaw infanticide? The pro-abortion argument demonstrates a deadly contradiction in its moral and ethical reasoning. They argue that the practices described in this bill do not happen and that we must not outlaw it. Indeed, some of the statements against the legislation exude an unparalleled level of insanity. Senator Patty Murray of Washington described the legislation as "clearly anti-doctor, anti-woman and anti-family." On what planet can lawmakers deem a bill that bans infanticide as "anti-family"?

Senator Murray continued, "It has no place becoming law. Its proponents claim it would make something illegal that is already illegal. [The legislation would] do nothing except help Republicans advance their goal of denying women their constitutionally protected rights."

The senator has erected a structure of one incompatible argument on another. If the bill set out to make something illegal that is already illegal, then why oppose the bill? If it is already illegal, then how would this law do anything to deny a woman's right to choose? Does this practice happen, or does it not happen? Sadly, it does happen.

The opinions against this bill look less like rational arguments grounded in reality and more like *Alice in Wonderland*—lunacy, fantasy, and a deep rabbit hole of deadly logic. Words no longer matter as pro-abortion advocates make every desperate, unfounded argument against a pro-life bill imaginable—even a bill that would have protected the life of a baby outside the womb. The same pattern of argument is rendered when politicians oppose laws that would outlaw abortions undertaken for reasons of sex-selection. They argue that it does not happen (when of course it does happen) and go on to argue that it would be wrong to outlaw the practice. When it comes to laws that would prevent abortions undertaken simply because of a diagnosis of Down syndrome, their argument changes. They admit that such abortions happen, but that a woman has the right to abort the baby anyway. Tragically, the vast majority of babies diagnosed with Down syndrome in the womb are now aborted. This is the nation we have become.

Some Took a Stand

Despite the failure of the Senate to pass a bill to ban infanticide, and despite the culture of death rising in places like New York, Rhode Island, Virginia, and Illinois, some states took a stand against the gathering storm over the sanctity of human life. The resilience of these states ought to encourage the pro-life movement—but the response from the pro-abortion movement, especially contenders for the Democratic nomination, demands attention.

In early 2019, the state of New York passed a new abortion bill that effectively legalized abortion right up until the moment of live birth. The new "Reproductive Health Act" even removed abortion altogether from the state's criminal law, meaning that the murder of a pregnant woman and her unborn child is now, in New York, only a single homicide—the murder of the unborn child is not considered murder at all. This is the deadly logic making its way through the states dominated by the pro-abortion movement. These states often fund abortions directly through Medicare programs or by other means. When the bill passed in the New York legislature, loud cheering broke out. The culture of death has cheerleaders.

Sadly, the developments in New York would be emulated by other states, including Illinois. The picture of abortion in the United States is now clear—a map of states that are increasingly pro-life and states that are even more abundantly pro-abortion. This great moral divide is now a political divide.

Several states have adopted important protections for unborn life. These laws—and the response to the laws—is a very revealing portrait of where we stand now in the United States. In keeping with his campaign promise, Governor Brian Kemp of Georgia signed into law the fetal heartbeat bill. This legislation prohibits abortions once doctors can detect the heartbeat of a child in its mother's womb—something detectable only six weeks into a mother's pregnancy. As we can expect, the measure provoked immediate backlash from the pro-abortion lobby.

The pro-abortion movement views heartbeat bills as a direct threat to the protections granted to women in the wake of *Roe v. Wade*, the Supreme Court decision that legalized abortions in the first trimester of pregnancy and for most of the second trimester. Thus, the fetal heartbeat bill prohibits abortions in the first trimester—something the pro-abortion movement simply will not tolerate.

Swift retribution came from every imaginable force for the pro-abortion agenda—politicians, political organizations, advocacy groups, and even Hollywood rushed to rebuke Georgia's heartbeat bill. Indeed, in the United States, the most powerful engine of cultural production and influence is arguably Hollywood, and the response of Hollywood to pro-life laws reveals the troubling vector of America's most powerful manufacturer of culture and morality.

CNN ran an article chronicling the open hostility of Hollywood elites to the Georgia law. According to CNN, actress Alyssa Milano "penned an open letter to Georgia House Speaker David Ralston and Governor Brian Kemp against the so-called heartbeat abortion bill. Dozens of other celebrities including Amy Schumer, Sean Penn,

Alec Baldwin, Don Cheadle, Rosie O'Donnell, Patton Oswalt, Sarah Silverman, and Mia Farrow signed the letter in support."[3]

Make no mistake: this is an act of overt coercion. The cultural elites issued a threat against the state of Georgia—if the state does not surrender and depart from its current course to protect the lives of unborn children, Hollywood will respond with the full force of its fury. Hollywood will pull out of Georgia, which would amount to an estimated loss of $2.7 billion for the state. According to the *Hollywood Reporter*, Georgia hosted 455 different film productions last year alone.

The Hollywood stars' letter states, "We want to stay in Georgia. We want to continue to support the wonderful people, businesses, and communities we've come to love in The Peach State. But we will not do so silently, and we will do everything in our power to move our industry to a safer state for women if [the bill] becomes law." The bill did become law, and Hollywood made good on its promise.

The open letter framed its moral imperative in the guise of "safety." Safety for whom? It is not safety for the living babies inside the womb. It is safety for the right of a woman to terminate the child inside of her—at every point, for any reason, paid in full.

Yet again, the moral revolutionaries have made the issue about the right of a woman with no regard to the child in her womb. They have erased the child from the moral equation. The only significant moral question is the woman and her autonomy over her body. For Hollywood, and for others of like mind, the baby doesn't exist.

The cultural bombardment of Georgia came not only from the actors and actresses but also from the writers behind them—namely, the Writer's Guild of America East and the Writer's Guild of America West. These two powerful entities joined in the coercive efforts, releasing a joint statement, which asserted, "This law would make Georgia an inhospitable place for those in the film and television industry to work, including our members. If the Georgia Legislature and Governor Kemp make [the bill] law, it is entirely possible that many of those in our industry will either want to leave the state or decide not to bring productions there. Such is the potential cost of a blatant attack on every woman's right to control her own body." This amounts to a full broadside by the cultural forces of modernity. The joint statement not only indicts Georgia for its policy proposal but makes it very clear that if Georgia moves forward, which it did, it will no longer serve as a suitable place to do business. Hollywood will have nothing to do with the state—or so it threatens.

Further retribution came as soon as Governor Kemp signed the bill into law. Toni Van Pelt, president of the National Organization for Women, issued a statement saying, "The fact is that women have a constitutional right to safe, legal abortion, and these alarming legislative machinations are part of a calculated and well-funded national effort to drum up political support for anti-abortion candidates in upcoming elections. Meanwhile, women's health, autonomy and their right to the pursuit of happiness are under serious threat." What morally atrocious age have we slipped into where we sacrifice babies on the altar of "women's health, autonomy, and their right to the pursuit of happiness"?

The heartbeat bills proposed in many states provoked America into a moral conversation about the life inside a mother's womb and the value inherit in that unborn child. George Will of the *Washington Post* wrote that proponents for the heartbeat bills aim to "provoke thinking about the moral dimension of extinguishing a being with a visibly beating heart."[4] Indeed, these bills do require us as a people to consider the moral veracity of silencing a beating heart. From a Christian worldview, we affirm the dignity of life at the moment of conception, not just six weeks into the pregnancy when a heartbeat is detected. *All* of life is sacred and worthy of protection. We should also note the extraordinary loyalty to which major media will go to avoid using the term "fetal heartbeat." The word "heartbeat" powerfully points to the humanity of the unborn child. It underlines the fact that the inhabitant of the womb *is a child.*

The *New York Times*, reporting on the re-election of John Bill Edwards as governor of Louisiana, noted that he had signed a bill "banning abortion after the pulsing of what becomes the fetus's heart."[5] In the same article covering the Louisiana law, the article referred to "embryonic pulsing." The secular media will do anything it can to avoid using the term "heartbeat"—that's the telling pattern. Yet again, the humanity of the unborn child is derided.

At the same time, this provocation brings out the worst of the pro-abortion lobby. Indeed, it shows the degeneracy of those willing to defend abortion at any cost. George Will cited a *New York Times* editorial from December 28, 2018, where the editorial board opposed the idea that "a fetus in the womb has the same rights as a fully formed person."[6]

This debate also brought out astounding comments from presidential candidates in the 2020 race. It turns out that this issue is not just about the woman's right to abort, but a theological issue. Make no mistake, every person is a theologian, even if that person is a United States senator from New York and formerly a contender for the Democratic nomination for president.

Senator Kirsten Gillibrand made that fact clear when she made a campaign stop in Georgia shortly after the heartbeat bill became law. During a panel discussion on abortion in light of this new law, theologian Gillibrand said that laws banning or restricting abortion are "against Christian faith." That's a statement that bears scrutiny.

To understand Senator Gillibrand's comment, it is important to remember that Senator Gillibrand has not always been as liberal on the issue as she is now. She was appointed to the Senate in 2009 when the seat was vacated by Hillary Rodham Clinton. When she was elected to Congress in 2006, Gillibrand was known as a Blue Dog Democrat, who even had a very high rating by the National Rifle Association. But ever since her appointment to the Senate, Gillibrand has been moving to the left.

Indeed, she has moved to the far left in her bid for the presidency, especially on the issue of abortion. She demanded that the United States government pass legislation that would remove the power from the states to restrict abortion in any way. She has also called for the dismissal of the Hyde Amendment, which guarantees that taxpayer money cannot be used to fund abortion. Furthermore, she has demanded the development of more abortion clinics and that abortion enjoy mandatory coverage from both private insurance plans and state plans, such as Medicaid. She also pledged that she would appoint only federal judges and Supreme Court justices who were committed to upholding *Roe v. Wade.*

Those proposals are typical these days of any Democratic candidate for any office in the nation. What was shocking was her injection of theology into the discussion when she said that laws banning or restricting abortion are "against Christian faith." Apparently, her argument is rooted in the doctrine of free will. She said, "If you are a person of the Christian faith, one of the tenets of our faith is free will. One of the tenets of our democracy is that we have a separation of church and state, and under no circumstances are we supposed to be imposing our faith on other people." That is theological nonsense. God did not create human beings as morally responsible creatures and then invite us to use those powers of choice in order to destroy unborn human life in the womb. The argument is absurd—but it is also deadly.

Senator Gillibrand attempted to say that the affirmation of human responsibility and the operation of the human will in decision-making means that we should be hands-off when it comes to legislation about abortion. She makes human will essentially sovereign in terms of moral responsibility. But how would this absolute moral freedom work in practice? Law exists to recognize human moral responsibility but also to put boundaries upon freedom. For example, it is against the law in every single state and every single nation to commit murder. It would be inconceivable to elevate free will to the point that a government would not place any restrictions upon its citizens to not commit murder.

There will always be ongoing political debates about the extent to which the law should bind the conscience and put boundaries on human behavior, but the essence of human society is built upon the existence of such laws. *Every* law restricts human freedom.

For Senator Gillibrand, the freedom of a woman to consider and choose abortion is an absolute freedom that no one should be able to restrict in any way. She essentially said that it is against the Christian faith to put any boundaries upon the decision-making of a woman considering abortion.

This argument is theological gibberish that leads to a deadly confusion. Embedded within the senator's argument is the claim that you can't legislate morality. She referred to the separation of church and state and said that abortion restrictions are an example of faith being imposed on other people. But there is always deep moral motivation behind every law. The question is, "Whose morality are we legislating?"

We are reminded that there are no non-theological people and there are, ultimately, no non-theological worldviews. The worldview may claim to be secular and non-theological, but even a secular worldview is theological in its rejection of theism. Indeed, every worldview has to determine how human society should be structured and ordered. Every society must answer the question of being. And, ultimately, every worldview must answer the question of what a human being is. The answer will always be theological, whether intended or not.

In 2018, the state of Alabama approved legislation that effectively outlawed abortion. Period. A last-minute negotiation provided a limited exemption for pregnancies that threaten a mother's life. That means that the bill did not secure exemptions for pregnancies as a result of rape or incest. Not long after the bill passed the Senate, Alabama governor Kay Ivey signed the legislation into law. Alabama's bold gesture marks a new chapter in the American chronicle of the abortion conflict.

Alabama, however, took an unprecedented leap by banning abortions outright. The proponents of the legislation strategically and intentionally positioned this sweeping ban on abortion as a challenge to the infamous 1973 Supreme Court case *Roe v. Wade*. This is a constitutional battle over the central question: Does the United States Constitution grant women the right to kill an unborn baby?

Pro-abortion advocates tried to dismiss this legislation from Alabama due to the gender makeup of the Alabama legislature. This sweeping ban on abortion was passed by a legislature made up of primarily male members. Indeed, in the Alabama Senate, of the thirty-five seats, thirty-one members are male. The argument of the pro-abortion movement, therefore, asserts that a group of men unilaterally decided what women can and cannot do with their bodies—this, by the pro-abortion estimation, is injustice.

This argument, however, fails to consider the makeup of the larger pro-life movement. The majority of people involved in the pro-life movement are not men but women. In June 2018, the Gallup organization released a poll revealing that women account for a larger percentage of the pro-life agenda—while the Alabama legislators are primarily men, the larger pro-life movement is represented by a majority of women. Poll after poll indicates that women are even more pro-life than men—which is, upon reflection, quite sensible. A woman is the first to have a relationship with the unborn baby within her.

During the debate, some legislators attempted to attach exemptions to the bill. Traditionally, three exemptions usually make their way into legislation that restricts abortions: risk to a woman's life, pregnancy caused by rape, or pregnancy caused by incest. The legislation signed into law in Alabama granted an exemption if the pregnancy risked the mother's life but not in cases of rape or incest. Each of these exemptions demand careful moral consideration.

First, very few pregnancies naturally threaten a mother's life. Moreover, the Christian worldview asserts that when a woman's life is at stake, it is not wrong to save her life. The intentional performing of an abortion is wrong, but not an abortion that occurs as an unavoidable situation to save the life of a mother under the trials of childbirth—threatening circumstances that are extremely rare.

An important caveat needs to be added, namely, that the woman's physical *life* must be at risk and not her *health*. The pro-abortion movement has strategically labeled abortive care as health care— thus, opposition to abortion amounts to opposing women's access to health-care services. The meaning, however, of health can include any number of definitions to suit the pro-abortion agenda. Health can refer to psychological or emotional health, which means that a woman, for any reason whatsoever, can abort her pregnancy.

The Alabama exemption, however, separates the *life* of a mother from the *health*. This is an important and crucial distinction that must be maintained.

The other two exemptions dealt with pregnancies resulting from rape or incest. Senators offered amendments to the Alabama bill in order to grant these exemptions—the measures failed. The debate over this issue is enormously significant and demands our attention.

If, after the moment of conception, a human life begins and develops, then at that very moment that life demands protection and care. *That* is the moral issue at stake, namely, the protection of unborn lives in the mother's womb. The ontological status of the unborn child is a paramount issue, and the personhood of the child is essential to human dignity—a dignity that cannot be erased or eroded by the pro-abortion movement. Inside the mother's womb from the moment of conception is a human life. That life should not and must not be destroyed.

The moral reality of the human life supersedes the *means* of how that human came into being. Rape and incest amount to gross acts of moral injustice and are indeed both sinful and illegal. These moral atrocities do unspeakable harm to women and assault their dignity. If a pregnancy results from rape or incest, the means of pregnancy is immoral but not the life now residing in the womb.

The Christian worldview, therefore, understands that there are no illegitimate children. All life is precious. All life is worthy of protection. Not even the most ardent pro-abortionist would dare argue that a child is illegitimate once born because of the circumstances of conception. The circumstances of conception, as horrifying and sinful as they are, in no way negate the ontological dignity and moral significance of the unborn child.

Over the decades, political reality has led many on the pro-life side to grant exemptions for rape and incest. Even before *Roe*, many on the pro-life side allowed for these exemptions in the hope that a pro-life consensus would permeate the morality of the country, effectively rendering the exemptions unnecessary.

Fury swiftly descended on Alabama, especially from the contenders for the 2020 Democratic nomination for president of the United States. As the *New York Times* reported, the measure's most forceful critics were the leading women candidates: Senator Kamala Harris of California, Senator Elizabeth Warren of Massachusetts, Senator Amy Klobuchar of Minnesota, and Senator Kirsten Gillibrand of New York, who has made fighting for women central to her campaign. Indeed, Senator Gillibrand tweeted, "This is a war on women, and it is time to fight like hell."

Moreover, in the wake of laws from states like Georgia and Alabama, Americans watched as Democrats took the stage in their first televised debate, where former HUD secretary Julián Castro stated, "I don't believe in only reproductive freedom, I believe in reproductive justice. All women—and that includes the trans community—have the right to an abortion." Apparently, the right to an abortion is so pervasive that it must now be guaranteed to a transgender woman—who, by the way, is biologically a male and utterly incapable of having children. The real argument here is that an individual identifying as a transgender *man*, though pregnant, is to be guaranteed an abortion. Just when we think the moral insanity of the pro-abortion argument has reached its limits, we now have candidates pushing the line even further.

Christians and the Sanctity of Human Life

We now stand at a watershed moment in American history. The year 2020 will go down in the books as a decisive year when the United States of America dealt with the challenge of abortion and the question of the sanctity of human life. These days, every national election is, in effect, a referendum or an abstention. Christians should note the troubling trends and pay careful attention to the deadly rhetoric of the pro-abortion movement. The culture of death seems to advance hour by hour in the United States—this is no mere political issue or policy debate; this is an issue dealing with real lives, real human beings, legally murdered on a massive scale. The events over the past year and this current political crisis serve as a moral MRI—a diagnostic test on the ethical condition of the United States. The current scans present us with a horrid diagnosis. The culture of death has metastasized and continues to spread across the nation.

This much is clear: American Christians must not only work and argue for the preservation of unborn life, but we must also pray for it. This is a defining moment for the moral character of the nation. It demands not only the attention of the finest intellectual and legal minds the nation has to offer but also the prayers of every Christian. May God have mercy and reverse the culture of death that has plagued this nation. May God help us to preserve and protect the life of every single human being—born and unborn.

The Christian witness demands that we present people, collectively and individually, with questions—questions that cause serious moral contemplation. The heartbeat bills, for example, are not just wholesome provocations—they are *holy* provocations. These bills procure a conversation wherein Christians can bear witness to the glory of the Creator by pointing to the development and beauty of human life in a mother's womb. Christians understand the weightiness of these debates. These are not merely public debates on a merely political issue—life and death are at stake; indeed, human life is at stake. That's why provoking conversation through heartbeat bills is a holy calling.

It is incumbent upon Christians to defend the sanctity of human life and confront the arguments demanding unfettered access to abortions. Abortion destroys countless human lives each and every year. We cannot be silent. The cries of dying children from the womb demand our utmost and zealous efforts to speak for them, defend them, and endeavor with all our might to eradicate abortion.

To do this, Christians must first and foremost pray. We pray for God to intervene, change hearts, and shed his mercy on a nation lost in the seas of secularism. We pray for ourselves: that God would grant us courage, conviction, and compassion—not only for the aborted children, but for many women who feel trapped, who see their only viable option as abortion.

Secondly, Christians must equip themselves with the Word of God to preach and proclaim the glory of humanity enshrined in God's creative mandate. Human beings at every stage of life, bear the image of God. To destroy image bearers intentionally is an act of high treason against the glory of our God who made man and woman in his image—an image that begins at conception. Christians need to contend for the sanctity of human life by equipping themselves with the powerful Word of the living God.

Finally, if all life is sacred, then Christians must champion adoption and foster care, and willingly step in to take on children who would have otherwise been aborted. Believers in Jesus Christ ought to be the leaders in the care of children. If we desire to see abortions end, then we must equally provide the necessary care to survivors of this abortion crisis.

The storm gathers, and it has already claimed the lives of millions of unborn children. We face a political, moral, and ethical crisis in this country—unless Christians press into the storm and declare the sanctity and dignity of human life, the casualties will be even more catastrophic. We cannot be silent. We cannot accept the logic of the culture of death. But the only real answer to the culture of death is the gospel of life.

FOUR

THE GATHERING STORM OVER MARRIAGE

"Dearly beloved, we are gathered here in the sight of God and in the face of this congregation, to join together this man and this woman in Holy Matrimony; which is an honorable state, instituted by God in the time of man's innocence, signifying unto us the mystical union that is betwixt Christ and his Church."

That familiar language from the Anglican Book of Common Prayer, recited thousands of times each week in various forms, presents a vision of marriage as a deeply Christian institution—even a necessary portrait of the love that unites Christ and his church. As marriage signifies this "mystical union," it points to an understanding that takes us far beyond the relationship of the husband and wife. Do most Christians have even the slightest understanding of this?

It is bad enough that the secular world has discounted marriage into a quasi-legal contract that, like other voluntary contracts, can be made or broken at will. The greater tragedy is the failure of Christians to take marriage seriously. According to the Bible, marriage is not only designed by the Creator as an arena for human happiness and the continuation of the human race—it is also the arena of God's glory, where the delights and disciplines of marriage point to the purpose for which human beings were made.

Marriage is about our happiness, our holiness, and our wholeness—but it is supremely about the glory of God. When marriage is entered rightly, when marriage vows are kept with purity, when all the goods of marriage are enjoyed in their proper place, God is glorified.

Our chief end is to glorify God, and marriage is a means of his greater glory. As sinners, we are all too concerned with our own pleasures, our own fulfillments, our own priorities, our own conception of marriage as a domestic arrangement. The ultimate purpose of marriage is the greater glory of God; and God is most greatly glorified when his gifts are rightly celebrated and received, and his covenants are rightly honored and pledged.

Marriage is not greatly respected in our postmodern culture. For many, the covenant of marriage has been discarded in favor of a contract of cohabitation. An ethic of personal autonomy has produced successive generations who think of the world as the arena of their own personal fulfillment and of marriage as an outdated relic of an outgrown culture of obligation.

Ours is an era of self-expression. Individuals express themselves through marriage, and then express themselves through divorce—as if all of life is nothing more than a succession of acts of self-expression.

A divorce culture explains away obligation and sacred promises as temporary statements of emotional disposition. I may *feel* married today—I may not *feel* married tomorrow.

Our culture is so sexually confused that the goods of sex are severed from the vows and obligations of marriage. Thanks to modern technologies, we can have sex without babies, babies without sex, and both without marriage. For many, marriage has become an irrelevancy.

For others it is worse. Some feminists have lambasted marriage as a domestic prison, a patriarchal and oppressive institution foisted upon unsuspecting men and women in order to deny them freedom, autonomy, fulfillment, and liberation. And, for a post-Christian culture, there is that nagging problem of the essential character of marriage as a sacred institution. A society that disbelieves in God will eventually disbelieve in marriage.

In addition to these challenges to marriage, the storm of the LGBTQ revolution gathers, demanding an entire reorientation of marriage and human relatedness. The sexual revolution rejects the Christian view of marriage and injects a new ethic into the equation, radically redefining an institution not made by humanity and for humanity but by God for our good and for his glory.

Christian couples who are committed to this high conception of marriage must see themselves as counter-revolutionaries. In a very real sense, they are. They are standing against the tide of public opinion, against the trend of modern morality, against the erosion of order and the deflationary market in faithfulness. Before God, they stand committed to each other and only to each other. To live together for each other, no matter what may come.

Procreation

Procreation and the nurture of children marks an essential pillar for God's design of marriage. Sometimes, infertility and miscarriages occur—a sign of the curse of sin on the world. These heartbreaking moments, however, do not diminish the God-designed order of pro-creation as a hallmark of marriage. Children are to be welcomed as gifts to the institution of marriage, transforming husband and wife into father and mother. In our anti-natalist age, some see children as impositions, or worse. The denial of a procreative orientation for marriage—every marriage genuinely open to the gift of children—is a denial of the biblical vision of marriage itself.

Numbers, however, paint a sad portrait for the state of child-bearing in America. Last year, the *Wall Street Journal* ran an editorial entitled "America's Millennial Baby Bust." As the paper reported, the US birth rate has hit a thirty-two-year low. During the period between 1960 and 2017, the US fertility rate (births per woman) was virtually cut in half. The dramatic fall in the fertility rate coincided with the development of the birth control pill.

Birth control and family planning gave rise to the idea of child-birth as merely an option—a plan in which one can choose or not choose to participate. For some, children are nothing more than inconveniences and leeches on time and money. Indeed, we live in a society where leaders call for unfettered access to abortions for any reason at any point in the pregnancy. Children in the womb are expendable, a commodity that can be terminated if it poses any inconvenience. We live in an age that belittles babies as accidental by-products of sexual passion.

Another argument, however, tries to connect a moral impera-tive *not* to have children with environmentalism. About ten years ago, a pair of scientists at Oregon State University published a study arguing that any effort to limit carbon emissions must consider the impact of reproductive choices on the ecological equation.

Paul A. Murtaugh and Michael G. Schlax made their case in "Reproduction and the Carbon Legacies of Individuals," published in the journal *Global Environmental Change*.[1] They argued, "While population growth is obviously a key component of projections of carbon emissions at a global level, there has been relatively little emphasis on the environmental consequences of the reproductive choices of an individual person." After all, there are not only the "immediate effects" caused by each offspring, but also the "additional impacts" if these offspring eventually produce further offspring.

According to the study, a female's decision to reproduce even a single child could have tremendous ecological effects. In order to make their case, the researchers traced a hypothetical single female's "genetic contribution to future generations" and projected the carbon legacy this contribution would entail. They posit that each child will add 9,441 metric tons of carbon dioxide to the carbon legacy of an average female.

To their credit, the researchers have invested considerable thought into exactly how they might project this "carbon legacy." They made their calculations with the understanding that children, both male and female, are likely to enter into reproductive pairs and produce future generations. They assumed a reproductive rate of 1.85 children per woman by the year 2050.

Taking all this into account, Murtaugh and Schlax estimated that a woman in the United States who makes significant lifestyle adjustments in order to reduce her own carbon legacy—such as increasing her car's fuel economy, reducing miles driven, adopting energy-efficient technologies, recycling, and so on—would save about 486 tons of carbon dioxide emissions over a lifetime. Yet, if you were to have two children, this would eventually add nearly forty times that amount of carbon dioxide to the atmosphere. In other words, all her efforts to be environmentally conscious and careful would be overwhelmed by her decision to have just two children.

The researchers argued:

> Clearly, an individual's reproductive choices can have a dramatic effect on the total carbon emissions ultimately attributable to his or her genetic lineage. Understanding the ways that an individual's daily activities influence emissions and explain the huge disparities in per capita emissions among countries is obviously essential, but ignoring the consequences of reproduction can lead to a serious underestimation of an individual's long-term impact on the global environment.

In one sense, a scientific report like this could represent little more than a hypothetical answer to a conjectured question.

Nevertheless, more is at stake here. These researchers made this point clear when, early in their article, they asserted: "Our basic premise is that a person is responsible for the carbon emissions of his descendants, weighted by their relatedness to him."

This is a quite remarkable assertion. While these two researchers have addressed their report to the scientific community, they openly acknowledge that their argument should be taken into consideration by those concerned with the policy challenge of climate change. As they argued, "Clearly, the potential savings from reduced reproduction are huge compared to the savings that can be achieved by changes in lifestyle."

Warnings that human reproduction will lead to ecological disaster have been common since at least the 1960s. Generally, these arguments have been couched in considerations of limited natural resources and environmental sustainability. Now, a new element is added to the mix, complete with a proposed model for quantifying a projected environmental impact. These two researchers advise that failing to take "reproductive choices" of individuals into account will effectively doom all other efforts to reduce the level of carbon emissions.

The logic of this argument is clear and chilling. The leap from scientific analysis to proposals for public policy is almost sure to come. How long will it be before prospective parents are warned that their decision to reproduce could be catastrophic for the environment? Should we now expect a cap and trade proposal for babies?

That idea may not be far off. Indeed, just last year, United States congresswoman Alexandria Ocasio-Cortez on her Instagram feed questioned the morality of parents considering having children. She stated,

Our planet is going to face disaster if we don't turn this ship around. And so it's basically like, there's scientific consensus that the lives of children are going to be very difficult and it does lead,

I think, young people, to have a legitimate question: Is it okay to still have children? Not just financially because people are graduating with $20,000, $30,000, $100,000 worth of student loan debt and so they can't even afford to have kids in the house. But also, just this basic moral question, like, "What do we do?"

Anti-natalist philosophies have been around even longer than arguments over ecology and sustainability. Given our biblical responsibility for environmental stewardship, Christians should indeed be thoughtfully engaged with the entire nexus of questions related to carbon emissions, climate change, and respect for the earth. Nevertheless, when we begin to measure babies in terms of a "carbon legacy" and a projected threat to the environment, we abandon the biblical worldview. Indeed, when it becomes a "basic moral question" over whether to have children or not, society has slipped into a vat of inexplicable chaos. Human beings cannot be reduced to a "carbon legacy," and the gift of children must never be seen as an assault upon the earth. Procreation is not a basic moral question or dilemma—it was designed by God as good, glorious, and indeed, part of the pre-fall, biblical mandate to be fruitful and multiply.

Back in the 1970s, we were warned that human civilization and the future of planet Earth was threatened by a "population explosion."[2] Paul Ehrlich, author of *The Population Bomb*, warned of mass starvation and the death of millions in the 1970s. It didn't happen, needless to say, but the intellectual class in the United States and Europe embraced a worldview that still attempts to reduce the human population by reducing births.

In reality, the great danger facing society is not having too many babies, but *too few*. Over a decade ago, the *New York Times* ran an article with the headline "No Babies?"[3] Then, in late 2019, the same paper ran another startling headline story, "The End of Babies."[4] In the United States, the birth rate has fallen dramatically, threatening the long-term national strength. In Europe, the picture is even more dramatic, with the total birth rate falling below population replacement, which points to an economic crisis. In the nation of Japan, the reality is actually catastrophic.

We are living in an age of human history in which having sex and having babies have been essentially separated. All this points to disaster, but it also underlines, graphically, the goodness of marriage as the gift God designed as the central unit of human society.

Indeed, the biblical worldview sends an unequivocal message that children are precious gifts to be received. They are not accidental by-products or intrusions upon our otherwise happy adult lives—to believe and behave so amounts to robbing God of his glory.

A Remedy Against Sin

In 1 Corinthians 7:2, 5, the apostle Paul wrote, "But because of the temptation to sexual immorality, each man should have his own wife and each woman her own husband. . . . Do not deprive one another . . . come together again, so that Satan may not tempt you because of your lack of self-control." The Corinthian church caused Paul concern due to their seduction by sexual sin and flagrant sexual immorality. Paul understood that sexual sins compromised the church's ability to represent Christ to Corinth. The apostle pointed to marriage as a means of channeling sexual desire into its proper context, lest believers "burn with passion" and sin against God (v. 9).

The secular storm, however, turned "burn[ing] with passion" into a hedonistic form of art. Explicit sexuality—stripped of the constraints of marriage—is the energy behind much of our economy, the material for our entertainment, and the best tool for advertising. Secularization corrupted the biblical sexual ethic and relegates the belief that sexual intercourse should be limited to marriage as an antiquated, moral throwback, hopelessly outdated. Secularism has paganized the culture. Pagans speak of holy things as if they were lowly while speaking of lowly things as if they were holy. The pagan mind worships the lowly things and disparages the holy things. The paganization of sex has robbed it of its glory, emptied it of its beauty, and maligned its God-ordained purpose as a grace enjoyed within the confines of the marriage covenant.

Indeed, for husbands and wives, the marriage covenant serves as a gracious reminder of a transcendent, pervasive love protecting the relationship between man and woman. A husband belongs to his wife and no other; a wife belongs to her husband and no other. God gives man and woman in marriage to share their passions together under the protection of the marriage covenant. This is not an oppressive system of the patriarch, nor is it a bygone socially constructed concept that guided humanity in times past from which we can now liberate ourselves. God designed sex to flourish under the care of the covenant between husband and wife.

The Christian worldview in no way impugns the desire for sex; but it must be a desire exercised and enjoyed properly within the marriage covenant. The world decries this idea as counterintuitive and countercultural. If we desire sex, then we must pursue the fulfillment of that desire, however we desire. The Scriptures, however, ground us in this guiding truth: the desire for sex is from God to drive us toward holiness in marriage. Under marriage, a husband and wife come together in covenantal unity, not viewing each other as a means of sexual satisfaction, but coming together in tender intimacy. Sex under the marriage covenant takes on its proper identity, namely, an adorned act protected by steadfast, committed love. When secularism breaches that identity and surrenders it to hedonistic passions, it diminishes the pleasure of this gift from God.

Regrettably, the church of Jesus Christ sometimes exhibits an unfaithfulness to this holy institution and this intimate relationship designed for husband and wife. Adultery plagues many Christian homes. It is an abomination in God's sight, for it disrupts the covenant professed by both spouses. It injects the relationship with anger, and fear, and erodes trust. Moreover, pornography poisons the screens of so many husbands, fathers, and their children. The plague is so contagious—it assaults non-Christians and entices many Christians to waste away in front of a screen, promising pleasure it cannot deliver. The sex drive, which should point toward covenant fidelity in marriage and all the goods associated with that most basic institution, has instead been corrupted to devastating effects.

Rather than directed toward fidelity, covenantal commitment, procreation, and the wonder of a one-flesh relationship, the sex drive has been degraded into a passion that robs God of his glory, celebrating the sensual at the expense of the spiritual, and setting what God had intended for good on a path that leads to destruction in the name of personal fulfillment. The most important answer we can give to pornography's rise in popularity is rooted in the Christian doctrine of sin. As sinners, we corrupt what God has perfectly designed for the good of his creatures, and we have turned sex into a carnival of orgiastic pleasures. Not only have we severed sex from marriage, but as a society, we now look at marriage as an imposition, chastity as an embarrassment, and sexual restraint as a psychological hang-up. The doctrine of sin explains why we have exchanged the glory of God for Sigmund Freud's concept of polymorphous perversity.

The postmodern age brought many wonders as well as incredible moral challenges. Often, technological achievement and moral complexity come hand in hand. This is most explicitly the case with the development of the internet. For the first time in human history, a teenager in his bedroom can encounter every imaginable sexual passion, perversion, and pleasure. Today's teenager, if not stranded on some desert island, is likely to know more about sex and its complexities than his father knew when he got married. Furthermore, what most generations have known only in the imagination—if at all—is now there for the viewing on websites, both commercial and free. The internet has brought an interstate highway of pornography into every community, with exit ramps at every terminal or personal computer.

Pornography represents one of the most insidious attacks upon the sanctity of marriage and the goodness of sex within the one-flesh relationship. The celebration of debauchery rather than purity, the elevation of genital pleasure over all other considerations, and the corruption of sexual energy through an inversion of the self, corrupts the idea of marriage, leads to incalculable harm, and subverts marriage and the marital bond.

Christians can stand against the sexual revolution through faithfulness in the marriage covenant—a testament to the world of the goodness of sex through God's created mandate. When Christians promote the biblical vision of sex under the covenant, they cast a brilliant light in the midst of this secular storm, which demands an unprecedented erotic liberty that will only ravage Western civilization. Christians can help society recapture the God-ordained glory of biblical sexuality by protecting the marriage bed and exuding sexual purity. Christian parents must instill in their children the biblical vision of sex as a gift properly enjoyed only in marriage. By holding fast to the biblical ethic regarding sex, Christians reveal the true splendor and glory of marriage.

Lifelong Companionship

The third great end of marriage is companionship throughout life, through good and bad, comfort and loss, sickness and health, until death parts the husband and wife. The mystery of completeness is expressed in the statement that the two shall become one. When a man and a woman exchange marriage vows, they become one solitary unit. After the exchange of these vows, we can no longer speak of the husband without the wife, or of the wife without the husband. They have become one, both in the physical union of the marital act and in the metaphysical union of the marital bond. As a married couple—husband and wife—they will live to the glory of God with each other, for each other, and to each other.

Indeed, in Genesis 2, God revealed that it was not good for Adam to live alone. In response, God declared in Genesis 2:18, "I will make him a helper fit for him." This divine declaration indicates that God exercised a creational mandate—Adam should not be left alone, and God himself would make Adam a helper to complement him. God then paraded every beast of the field and every bird of the heavens in front of Adam. Adam inspected and named every animal, realizing that from the entire creation, there was no helper fit for him. Nothing complemented him.

In verse 21, God caused a deep sleep to fall on Adam; while he slept, God removed one of Adam's ribs and fashioned Eve. The next morning, God brought Eve to Adam, and Adam exclaimed, "This at last is bone of my bones and flesh of my flesh; she shall be called Woman, because she was taken out of Man" (v. 23). The verse rings with a sigh of relief, joy, and gladness—after Adam had seen all of creation, he now at last, by God's grace, was joined together with his wife. Indeed, the chapter concludes with God's sovereign declaration: "Therefore a man shall leave his father and his mother and hold fast to his wife, and they shall become one flesh" (v. 24).

The narrative of Genesis 2 is rich with theological significance. It is a narrative that Christians desperately need to recapture so that we might face the secular storm. First, Genesis 2 reveals that the companionship of marriage amounts to nothing less than a divine ordinance. Marriage is not merely a human invention that underwent a process of sociological adaptation. Social evolution did not create marriage. The companionship between husband and wife, male and female, was no accident.

This truth directly contradicts this secular age. Our society has reduced marriage to a socially constructed commodity—malleable to personal and cultural convenience. Indeed, when the Supreme

Court legalized same-sex marriage in 2015, Chief Justice John Roberts rightly identified the drastic and unprecedented actions taken by the Court—the Court completely "redefine[d] marriage," with the majority's decision amounting to "an act of will, not a legal judgment."[5] In the aftermath of the *Obergefell* decision, society continues down the chaotic spiral of marital subjectivism, where transcendent and ontological realities no longer define marriage.

Second, God enshrined in the marriage union the concept of complementarianism, which upholds the equal dignity of man and woman as both created in the image of God but complementing one another through different gender roles. This means obeying the Bible's clear teachings on male leadership in the home and in the church. Indeed, as the Genesis narrative makes clear, gender is not incidental. It is essential and part of God's original design to make marriage for his glory. The needs shared between husband and wife are to God's glory. The satisfaction of the woman in the man's eye is to God's glory. The satisfaction and pleasures enjoyed between husband and wife praise God's glory. The commonality of living our life together as husband and wife in sickness and in health, till death they do part is God's glory. This one flesh relationship is to God's glory, and it is a relationship between one man and one woman, complementing each other in their respective, God-ordained roles as husband and wife.

The previous paragraph haunts post-modernity and the rising tides of secularism. This biblical attestation collides with the sexual revolution, which decries any attempt to see women live as women and men to live as men. The message is plain—men and women must redefine masculinity and femininity to comport with the new secular definitions, which attempt to abrogate the God-glorifying roles of husbands as husbands and wives as wives, men as men and women as women.

The assaults on gender, which will be taken up substantively in chapter 6, cannot be dismissed as a minor development in this secular age. The attempts to redefine gender as unimportant, and a created tool of men to suppress women demeans and defames the will of the glorious, gracious God of the universe who made men and women with distinctive roles—not as a form of punishment or in any way attempting to degrade a particular sex. Indeed, as the society tries to liberate itself from the verity and virtue of gender, it only sows greater confusion, consternation, and chaos. Living outside God's designs portends only to destruction. Christians, therefore, must endeavor in every way to recapture the glory of gender in the marriage covenant. The biblical doctrine of complementarianism, far from oppressing any gender in the marriage, promotes flourishing between spouses who live in accordance with and under God's instruction.

The third theological truth affirmed in Genesis 2 pertains to the one flesh relationship God established between Adam and Eve—a relationship of holding fast to each other, of never forsaking each other. Jesus explained this reality in Mark 10:8–9, proclaiming that husband and wife "are no longer two but one flesh. What therefore God has joined together, let not man separate." In other words, marriage ought to be a lifelong commitment between husband and wife. Marriage is not a contract that either party can renege. Instead, it is a covenant.

Despite this reality, divorce casts its dark, harrowing shadow over Western civilization and especially within the church of Jesus Christ. Divorce marks the clearest example of the canonization of the church. Far too many homes that bear the name of Christ suffer from disastrous divorces, which leave in their wake broken homes, traumatized children, and a defamation of the marriage union. We are witnessing a divorce revolution that not only made marriage a tentative, if not temporary, condition, but also redefined marriage as nothing more than a public celebration of an essentially nonnegotiable individual act of self-expression. Divorce became commonplace in America and is no longer considered a major moral problem in our cultural conversation—but of course, it is.

If you trace the trajectory of the sexual revolution, rampant, no-fault divorce preceded same-sex marriage. When divorce reigned as the new normal for marriages, it redefined the institution as a covenant amounting to a public commitment for a lifetime. Once the society remade marriage into a morally irrelevant, non-binding commitment, it was just a short jump to same-sex marriage. If a culture can dismiss the covenant of marriage, it can dismiss every other binding, biblical, and indeed, glorious commitment, which made marriage a beautiful, God-glorifying reality.

Conclusion

Why is all of this so important? A stable and functional culture requires the establishment of stable marriages and the nurturing of families. Without a healthy marriage and family life as foundation, no lasting and healthy community can long survive.

Christians must contend for marriage as God's gift to humanity—a gift central and essential to human flourishing and a gift that is limited to the conjugal union of a man and woman—a union that lasts for a lifetime. We cannot be silent, and we cannot join the moral revolution that stands in direct opposition to what we believe the Creator has designed, given, and intended for us and for his glory. We cannot fail to contend for marriage as a holy institution, made up of one man and one woman, who pursue each other in a monogamous, covenantal union.

Our Christian responsibility cannot be overstated in the midst of this secular storm. We are charged to uphold the biblical vision of marriage—we uphold it by living it. It is incumbent upon Christians to show the world the glory of marriage so that pornography is inconceivable, divorce eradicated from our vocabulary, and same-sex marriage unthinkable. When Christians, under the covenant of marriage, guided by the Holy Spirit, stand upon the unassailable

Word of God, they display the beauty of marriage. When Christians build their marriages upon the biblical foundations, they display as the apostle Paul said in Ephesians 5, the mystery of the gospel of Jesus Christ.

The secular storm gathers over marriage. It devastates families and wrenches parents from their children. It disrupts a love which ought never end. But Christians can press on as a light in the midst of deep cultural confusion to declare to the world God's glory through the glory of marriage.

FIVE

THE GATHERING STORM OVER THE FAMILY

Back in 1977, the brilliant cultural observer Christopher Lasch published a book with a remarkable title, *Haven in a Heartless World: The Family Besieged.*[1] The title told the story—the family was already in big trouble. Interestingly, Lasch's argument was that the family was necessary as an oasis of security and warmth in a world growing even colder in the advance of a technological age. But the family was being crushed by modernity, Lasch saw. Similarly, sociologists Peter and Brigitte Berger warned about "the War on the Family," and they described how the family unit was being subverted by everything from economic pressures to government encroachment.[2]

Christopher Lasch's book came out the year I graduated from high school. The Bergers' book released just six years later. They had no idea what was coming, and how the family would be further endangered in the next few decades.

I cannot explain my life without my parents and family. Who I am today stems from God's grace in my mother and father. Their love, dedication, and Christ-centered parenting nourished my upbringing. Moreover, I would not be who I am without my own family. My children taught me so much and filled me with years of plentiful joy—a joy that only multiplies now with my grandchildren. Most important is my wife, Mary, who is without a doubt one of God's greatest blessings in my life.

God intended families for this kind of joy and security. Indeed, family life, much like marriage, was no accident. God established the family unit from the beginning, commanding Adam and Eve to be fruitful and multiply. God extends the familial language throughout the Scriptures, where it finds its fulfillment in the family of the living God, founded through the sacrifice of Jesus Christ. Through Jesus' atonement, he initiated a new family—an eternal family of brothers and sisters in Christ who will dwell with God for all eternity. Far from a social construct, families display the grace of God, the glory of the gospel, and are essential for any functioning society.

Secularization, however, cannot and will not tolerate the biblical worldview on any matter or issue. Indeed, the secular storm not only threatens issues of public policy like religious liberty, abortion access, and marital laws, but also levies a full broadside into private homes. The forces of modern "progress" mount an offensive even against the family unit because the future disciples of the new worldview are our children. For an increasingly hostile secular culture to claim total dominance, it must eradicate any semblance or scent of a pre-modern or biblical worldview in the upbringing of the future generation.

The End of Parental Rights

The push of a secular worldview erodes the roles of parents in the upbringing of their children. Case after case, story after story, chronicles the downgrade of parental rights—secularism subverts the authority of parents who refuse to sing its seductive tune. If parents object to secularization, then they must be removed from the equation.

The following are examples of the moral calamities facing a Western civilization that no longer cherishes the family.

Chaos in Canada

Just last year, the world seemed to sleep as the Supreme Court of British Columbia ordered that a fourteen-year-old girl receive testosterone injections without parental consent. The court declared that if either of her parents referred to her using female pronouns or addressed her by her birth name, the parents could be charged with family violence.

Jeremiah Keenan, reporter for the *Federalist*, documented this horrifying tale of moral chaos.[3] Evidently, the girl's school counselor encouraged her to identify as a boy as early as the seventh grade. When the child turned thirteen, her doctor and his colleagues at the British Columbia Children's Hospital decided that she "should begin taking testosterone injections in order to develop a more masculine appearance." Keenan reported that while the mother accepted the idea of hormone injections, the girl's father was "concerned about the permanent ramifications of cross-sex hormones." Further: "Suspecting that his daughter's mental health issues might be more of the cause than the effect of her gender dysphoria, he ultimately decided that it would be better for her to wait until she was older before she embarked on any irreversible course of treatment."

Despite the father's concerns and rights as a parent, the doctor informed the parents that hormone treatments would commence simply based on the expressed consent of the child and the agreement of doctors. The lead doctor claimed that he had the right to usurp parental control due to prevailing law in British Columbia known as the Infants' Act. When the father sought an injunction from the court in British Columbia, a judge deemed that the daughter was empowered with "consent to medical treatment for gender dysphoria." The father responded to the court's decision, stating,

"The government has taken over my parental rights. They're using [my daughter] like she's a guinea pig in an experiment."

The father continued in his outrage, asking, "Is the British Columbia Children's Hospital going to be there in 5 years when she rejects her male identity? No, they're not. They don't care. They want numbers." Keenan aptly reported that the majority of children diagnosed by sex change clinics with gender dysphoria or gender identity disorder have actually returned to identify with their gender assigned at birth.

The sexual revolutionaries are scandalously dishonest about the consequences or implications of their worldview. Indeed, the father reflected on transgender clinics in England that, due to enormous activist pressure, fast-track children into transition treatments. The father commented, "These activists are taking over and it's not in the interest of our kids. It's in the interest of self-promotion and the things that they want to do and accomplish."

Indeed, the secular storm and the sexual revolution aim to normalize its entire transgender ideology. The LGBTQ revolutionaries have chipped away at the moral foundation of society—by opening the door to adult gender dysphoria, it would only be a matter of time before they extended their logic to young children who should have access to hormonal treatments and gender reversal medical procedures. No matter how hard they try, however, the sexual revolutionaries have no way to normalize what they propose for children. There is no way to look at this story without serious moral concern and outrage; an outrage directed not only at the indoctrination of young minds but also at the disavowal of parental rights.

This story out of Canada reveals the deeply subversive aims of the sexual revolutionaries and their agenda—they now target the rights of parents; they disrupt the life of the home and subvert familial bonds. The court's decision in British Columbia opened the door to the nullification of all parental rights—the child, no matter the age, is increasingly considered to be autonomous. Children and teenagers, guided and advised and even pushed by activists and medical authorities, can decide what to do with their bodies. Not only that, if the parents dare to refer to their transgender child by their actual biological sex, the parents can be charged with violating the family violence laws.

This is not a twisted fantasy novel. It is a real case, with real people, with a real judge, and with massively real consequences.

A moral reorientation of society occurs when the revolutionaries enact the logical and consistent implications of their worldview. For the sexual revolution, it began with claims that, for adults, gender is merely a social construct and gender identity is up to the individual. But if that logic applies to adults, it will inevitably apply to adolescents and children as well. The fluidity of gender and its deconstruction as a fixed, moral norm must extend to every person at every age. Every individual, they argue, even little children, must possess legally protected autonomy to decide their gender identity, declare it, and seek hormonal treatments and more.

When that logic infects a society, moral absolutes disappear. In Canada, the sexual revolution has sacrificed parental rights on the altar of a perverse moral ideology.

Like a destructive tidal wave, the moral revolution crushes the norms and moral structures that have guided human civilization for thousands of years. In this secular moment, parents no longer serve as the responsible authorities for the nurturing of their children but are obstacles that must be removed.

Indeed, the sexual revolution continuously seeks to undermine parental authority as evidenced by another case in Alberta. Jill Croteau for *Global News* reported a story with the headline "Gay-Straight Alliance Law Challenged at Alberta Court of Appeal."[4] Croteau wrote, "A court of appeal heard both sides on the impacts of gay-straight alliances in schools. While one side argues they limit a parent's right to know, the other says it protects children whose parents may not accept their sexual identity."

The substance of this issue centers around schools that refer students to gay-straight alliances, or clubs, without divulging that information to parents. Indeed, some schools will place students with an openly gay or LGBTQ counselor without ever notifying the parents. These students will receive encouragement to accept a gay identity—conversations that go on while parents remain oblivious and intentionally left in the dark.

The forces of secularism and the moral revolutionaries have pressed an agenda the logic of which is clear: parents who refuse to get on board must be severed from their children. A moral meltdown has occurred.

Fiasco in France

Secularism's tactic aims not only to subvert the relationship between children and their parents but also to sow moral confusion into the minds of children. When God created human beings, he made them rational creatures with the capacity to think, reason, and make logical conclusions. After the fall in Genesis 3, that capacity succumbed to the effects of sin, making humans less rational than God created—we do not see the obvious and reasoning trends away from God and his goodness. Though human reason suffers from the ravages of sin, it remains part of what it means to be made in God's image. As such, humans will, over time, become consistent in their thoughts and actions.

Recent events in France display this rational consistency—the inevitability of A leading to B. Given the effects of sin, that consistency typically makes a downward spiral into further chaos and moral confusion.

Recently, *Newsweek* ran a story with the headline "'Mother' and 'Father' Replaced with 'Parent 1' and 'Parent 2' in French Schools Under Same-Sex Amendment." Callum Paton, reporter for *Newsweek*, wrote, "France's National Assembly has voted in favor of an amendment removing the terms *mother* and *father* from forms in the nation schools. Instead using the terms 'parent 1' and 'parent 2.' The amendment which passed into law alongside a new school bill Tuesday has been seen by France's majority party as a necessary step to bring France's schools into line with the European Nations 2013 same sex marriage law."[5]

This story powerfully illustrates the unavoidable logic of the secular storm. When society pushes on one domino, the rest fall in suit.

In 2013, France legalized same-sex marriage. That law, however, was inconsistent with other societal structures like school forms, which had labels for a child's "mother" and "father." Now, the consistency of the same-sex marriage ethic has reached into France's school system, redefining "mother" and "father" as "parent 1" and "parent 2." Throughout French history, every child was assumed to have a mother and a father. The logic of same-sex marriage, however, requires a society to jettison tradition (and, for that matter, reason) for the mores of the sexual revolution. In the wake of same-sex marriage, a child could have two moms or two dads, which means the school forms were outdated and belonged to the antiquated tradition of the dark ages.

Even though this new regulation is consistent with France's same-sex marriage law from 2013, the change of school forms has been controversial. *Newsweek* reports that, at best, 95 percent of families in France are made up of children with a mother and a father. Such a staggering figure obviates the need to change the school forms to "parent 1" and "parent 2."

Furthermore, the French realize that this minor change on a school form has enormous moral consequences. These changes trade one system of morality for another. It is a radical redefinition of the family. Even though France exudes a notorious liberal attitude on a plethora of moral and social issues, they comprehend the sweeping implications of this new mandate from the French government. One French lawmaker told *Newsweek* that re-designating parents as "parent 1" and "parent 2" is a fantasy. *Newsweek* reported, "He added that he felt the negotiation of gender would deconstruct the balance of society." Indeed, that is exactly what the moral revolutionaries endeavor to attain.

Language really matters. The use of language serves as a moral signal, and the moral revolutionaries understand the power of language and the influence words carry. The sexual revolution insists that society must alter its use of language and terms to accommodate its moral agenda. Indeed, we can fully expect that the revolutionaries have only just begun—they will demand more and expect society to either get in line or get out of the way.

Christians need to look at the news coming out of France with honest heartbreak. This isn't about a school form, but the dismantling of a society's most basic structure. The moral revolution has demolished the family unit, redefined it out of existence. Yet this institution is established in the very beginning of the Bible. At the end of Genesis 2, we are told that "a man shall leave his father and his mother and hold fast to his wife, and they shall become one flesh" (v. 24). God established at the onset of his creation the union between one man and one woman. God, in the goodness of his creation, formed the family unit—a family that also brings about the joy of children as extensions of God's grace and love. These children were never intended to look on their parents as merely "parent 1" and "parent 2," but as "mother" and "father." To reject "mother" and "father" is not only a repudiation of the biblical worldview, but a rejection of the God who ordered his creation perfectly and to his glory.

Secularism sets out to redefine humanity. This new law in France isn't just the revision of a school form; it attempts to reconstruct humanity altogether. "Mother" and "father" are now artifacts in France—labels that must be dispensed with in the new moral order of the sexual revolution. And the revolution will not stop here. It will do all it can to bring every dimension of every society into consistency with its moral demands, no matter how costly those demands.

Breakdown in Britain

Indeed, the cost of secularism's demands erupted in England with the United Kingdom's government-initiated plans to control the education of all children, particularly children homeschooled by their parents. Ruth Woodcraft of *Evangelical Now* reported, "The government is now consulting on new plans for a home education register. But this isn't about home education; it's about the right of any parent to teach their child anything."[6]

This move marks a plan in Britain to register homeschool children in an attempt to intervene in the relationship between parents and their children. As Woodcraft argues, it is only a small jump "to tell parents how and what can be said at home on other matters. As suspicion of faith increases, it would only be a small stop to see Bible teaching brought into the government's sights." Her conclusion might sound like a slippery-slope argument. After all, isn't it incumbent upon governments to register homeschooled children to make sure that all children have access to a good and solid education?

Woodcraft, however, makes a clear and pointed argument that reveals the trajectory of this new proposal by Britain. She wrote,

> The register was first suggested in the *Casey Review.* That report had a prejudicial attitude towards religion throughout. Mainstream views on sexual ethics were referred to as regressive, and Christians were seen as part of the problem for a lack of integration in society. The assumption in the consultation is that a child's development, as defined by the government, could be damaged by parents teaching children. Evangelical Christians are mentioned in one of the impact documents to be read alongside the survey, as an increasing number home educate.

The implications of Britain's move are enormous and will end in disaster. The right to educate our children is a fundamental parental right—a right now questioned by the moral and secular revolution. If the forces of secularization desire a worldview revolution, then it will endeavor to capture the minds of children and the coming generations. Secularism will not tolerate, by its estimation, parents "brainwashing" their children with nonsensical and harmful dogmas like a biblical worldview.

This reality points to the reason secularization set its gaze on public education. Indeed, Americans need only to look in their own backyard to see the advances of the secular age in education. School districts in California and Colorado are considering a sex education regimen in lockstep with the LGBTQ revolutionaries. Moreover, some school districts now prohibit teachers and school employees from informing parents if their children decide to join LGBTQ clubs. The dissemination of secularization accelerates when it dominates the hearts and minds of children.

It is no surprise, therefore, to learn that Britain has now set its gaze on institutions of private education, currently outside the grip of the state. The schools outside the control of the secular revolution must be brought in line. Amazingly, Woodcraft cited in her article that in Great Britain, "home education has grown 40% in the last three years." This is an astounding increase, pointing to the moral concern among many parents in England.

Woodcraft cited a report known as the Casey Review, a report dedicated to reviewing the integration and opportunity in isolated and deprived communities for education. The report states, "It is extremely concerning that children can be excluded from mainstream education without sufficient checks on their wellbeing and integration. The Government should step up the safeguarding arrangements for children who are removed from mainstream education, and in particular those who do not commence mainstream schooling at all."

This straightforward statement makes certain that children who remain outside the mainstream of government education must be reached and integrated into Britain's overall educational vision. Moreover, the report couches its assertions in moral terms—it is a concern that children could receive an education from their parents outside the "mainstream" of education.

The report goes on to state that children outside the mainstream must be registered with the local authorities. It is, moreover, the duty of the authorities to ensure that children receive an adequate, mainstream education devoid of any "divisive practices." Then, the report suggests,

> Parents should continue to have the right to home educate their children but stronger safeguards are required to ensure the child's right to a decent and suitable education for life in Britain, and to protect them from harm. The evidence we have seen in this review shows it is too easy for children to be raised in a totally secluded environment that does not provide a suitable education or sufficient protection from harm.

Again, this report makes glaringly moral claims. Parent-child education is seen as harmful in the eyes of this report. Indeed, the parent might seclude a child from the mainstream ideologies of public education, which means that parents could prevent their children from accepting the mainstream moral judgments of this secular age.

The report explicitly states that, of particular concern, is religious education outside the "mainstream" of English society. The report declares, "At the same time there has been a shift away from mainstream Christian denominations and a growth in evangelical and Pentecostal churches." The Casey Review does not come right out and say that Christian homeschooling must end—but it does point in that direction through the use of language like "mainstream." The report believes that it is harmful to children to receive an education outside the mainstream of society; and the report does make clear that evangelicalism is, in fact, outside the mainstream.

Moreover, the report argues,

> While many people in the UK appear to be seeing religion as increasingly less important and, in some cases, less of a force for good, for others religion is very important in their daily lives. Within this latter group there appear to be some who are keen to take religion backwards and away from 21st Century British values and laws on issues such as gender equality and sexual orientation; creating segregation and pulling communities apart.

Right here, in a government report, readers find massively theological arguments. The report states that those who believe religion to play an important role in their daily lives hold to specious, backwards, and antiquated religious sentiments harmful for society. They are not in line with British values. They will split communities up and cause irreparable harm. To believe that marriage is between one man and one woman, or to believe that boys—as they have been known throughout human history—are boys, and that girls are girls, is depicted not only as pigheaded but as potentially violent to societal peace. The state must intervene and stamp out any educational practices that promote visions of human flourishing divergent from secular orthodoxy.

The Erosion of the Parent

These cases from Canada, France, and England all represent the trajectory of this secular storm. The secular age will not tolerate worldviews that challenge its comprehensive vision for humanity. Parents who refuse to get in line with the moral revolutionaries will soon find themselves childless or displaced, as the state intervenes to rescue children from the dangerous and backward beliefs of their Christian parents.

These moves taken by Canada, France, and England will not stay there—typically, these nations outpace the United States in secularization by only a few years. These headlines will soon describe American cities and states. Indeed, California has already initiated a process of reviewing homeschooled children. It will not be long before these developments appear on the American landscape.

The assault on the relationship between a parent and child is not merely an assault on some socially constructed tool that was once useful for humanity. The family—and the role and authority of parents—was established by God himself. The Creator of the universe crafted the parent-child relationship as an institution for human good and flourishing; it promotes love, relationships, and societal peace. As such, this is a sacred relationship, grounded in an ontological truth, enshrined in the creational order itself.

These stories also point to this tragic reality: faithfulness to Christian teaching now places parents outside the mainstream and could potentially lead to a termination of parental rights. Because Christians will not succumb to the demands of the sexual and secular revolution, the revolution now assaults the sacred bonds between a parent and a child. This is a zero-tolerance war that the moral revolutionaries will not surrender—the battle for the hearts and minds of children is too valuable for the revolutionaries to neglect.

Christians need to understand what is at stake. The end of parental rights is the end of the family, and eventually, the end of human civilization as we know it. The logic of the secular age must be met with the full force of Christian conviction, witness, and worldview.

Back in 1977, Christopher Lasch saw that the family served to mediate and lessen the pressure of an ever-encroaching external world constituted by government. He saw the family as threatened, and he understood that parents were increasingly seen by the architects of the new society as part of the problem. Even then, the role of parents was being undermined, but with more subtlety.

Lasch concluded his book with this announcement:

> The citizen's entire existence has now been subjected to social direction, increasingly unmediated by the family or other institutions to which the work of socialization was once confined. Society itself has taken over socialization or subjected family socialization to increasingly effective control. Having thereby weakened the capacity for self-direction and self-control, it has undermined one of the principal sources of social cohesion, only to create new ones more constricting than the old, and ultimately more devastating in their impact on personal freedom.[7]

That was 1977. Lasch could not have imagined where we now stand four decades later. But we can, and we must realize that the family will effectively disappear and parents will be silenced.

This moral revolution progresses by redefining institution after institution, relationship after relationship. The revolution has redefined the institution of marriage already—now, it sets its gaze on the relationships between father and son, mother and daughter. These relationships, in the eyes of secularists, are expendable. If it does not serve the revolution, it must cease to exist.

SIX

THE GATHERING STORM OVER GENDER AND SEXUALITY

The church of Jesus Christ faces an unprecedented challenge: the collision between it and a new sexual ethic, a collision between *revelation* and *revolution*. The revolution is a sexual one, and it is indeed a revolution, demanding a complete reordering of society and civilization. Indeed, this revolution questions a fundamental grounding of what it means to be human—to be male and female. The sexual revolution usurps the very source and ground of human identity, right down to whether or not our creation determines, in any sense, who we are as humanity. Moreover, this revolution rejects the revelation of God and his creational mandates—the goodness with which he designed sex, maleness, and femaleness.

The progress of this revolution did not occur randomly. What follows is an account of how we got to where we find ourselves today. Much of the sexual revolution began when scientists developed technology aimed at liberating human sexuality from reproduction. The single greatest impetus of the sexual revolution was the advent of birth control, which began to transform the notion of the "possible" and gave way to an onslaught of consequences no one saw coming. There is no way to overestimate the impact made—indeed, the energy released that fueled the sexual revolution—by the advent of the oral contraceptive.

Contraception and the Sexual Revolution

The sexual revolution was impossible until the advent of modern birth control. How can you have a sexual revolution when sexual intercourse remains inherently bound to procreation? The bonds of human relationship and the reality of familial obligations squelched the full manifestation of the sexual revolution. Furthermore, unity of sex with procreation stifled any widespread notion that human beings are anything but male and female. Contraception, however, severed the union between sex and procreation, giving rise not only to a pandemic of sexual intercourse outside the boundaries of marriage but also to the reimagining of human sexuality and gender. For the sexual revolutionaries, contraception liberated humanity from the oppressive chains of the biblical worldview and morality, which guided much of Western civilization for centuries. As humanity began to alter the sacred, precious, and most intimate expression of love between husband and wife, it set the culture on a pathway to total sexual revolution. When children became an entirely avoidable option, then sexual expression radically expanded, multiplied, and overthrew all constraints.

The introduction of contraception in the 1960s began to redefine the notion of marriage as an indissoluble union between a man and woman. When the solemnity and sacredness of sex was diminished, the lifelong *covenant* of marriage was downgraded to the temporary *contract* of marriage. Removing the possibility of pregnancy re-created marriage from a covenant relationship into just a really long date with residential benefits. There is no wonder, therefore, why divorce rates skyrocketed—the society, and indeed, the church did little to stem the tide or reverse this downward trend. Divorce, like the pill, came to the culture as a gift of liberation.

Not long after the introduction of contraception, the Supreme Court legalized abortion across the entire United States in 1973. If the pill separated sex and procreation, abortion separated pregnancy and responsibility. Now, not only could we prevent pregnancy, but unwanted children could easily be discarded and eliminated. The sexual revolution sacrificed the sanctity of human life on the altar of sexual progression and liberation.

By the 1970s, we could see a full-blown revolution that began with the massive worldview shifts in the wake of oral contraception. Indeed, by the early years of the 1970s, a full-scale sexual revolution was underway, and it began with a riot at the Stonewall Inn.

The Rise of the Gay Rights Movement

On June 28, 1969, the police in New York City's Greenwich Village raided a gay bar, the Stonewall Inn. What made history, however, was the protest that ensued. Though attempts had been made to legalize same-sex relationships before 1969, the Stonewall riots marked a pivotal turning point for the gay rights movement.

On the fiftieth anniversary of the Stonewall riots, Moisés Kaufman, a gay literary figure in the United States, wrote an article for the *New York Times* reflecting on the gay rights movement. He wrote,

> One of the most important achievements of the Stonewall uprising was that it began a radical redefinition of the character of the LGBTQ person in the popular imagination. In 1969, homosexuality was still defined as a mental illness by the medical profession and same-sex relations were a crime in 49 states. The uprising showed the world a new image of our community. We

were no longer willing to hide in closets in silence and shame. We would take to the streets and demand to be full citizens. Within months, several activist groups like the Gay Liberation Front, the Gay Activists Alliance and the Street Transvestites Action Revolutionaries were formed.[1]

The Stonewall riots added gas to an already smoldering flame— the protest moved the gay rights movement into the public arena. Indeed, just a year after the Stonewall riots, New York City had its first gay pride parade with other cities following suit. Those parades are now a staple in American public life.

Reflecting on Stonewall, Kaufman concluded,

Today, the building that houses the Stonewall Inn has earned a listing in the National Register of Historical Places. . . . Homosexuality has been decriminalized nationwide. Lesbians, gay men and bisexuals are able to serve openly in the military. There's federal hate crime protection and AIDS has become a chronic illness as opposed to a fatal one. . . . We have marriage equality, and a gay man is making a serious run for the presidency. In this context, the celebration of the 50-year anniversary of Stonewall may feel euphoric. But is euphoria the right attitude for this moment in time? It is always tempting when writing the history of minorities to focus on the victories. But for all of these achievements, in 28 states employment discrimination based on sexual orientation and gender identity or expression is still legal. That means you can get married on Sunday and get fired on Monday.[2]

In Kaufman's view serious challenges still face the LGBTQ movement, even fifty years after the Stonewall riots. According to Kaufman, the gay community, though celebratory of Stonewall, must consider the battles still being waged, and the fight still ahead. He then described the nature of the conflict with the following words: "The greatest battle being fought in the hearts and minds of Americans is between the enlightenment ideals that gave birth to our democracy, and the autocratic repressive views that threaten progress."[3] That language is absolutely striking.

Stonewall was only the beginning. The sexual revolution is far from over. The gay rights movement continues to reorient the moral fabric of Western civilization. The LGBTQ revolution demands not only equality but also the suppression of divergent worldviews, namely, the Christian worldview. Any moral code that denies the new sexual rights must be silenced, for, in Kaufman's words, the worldview is nothing more than the vestige of an authoritarian system of oppression. These words come not as friendly debate and discourse over moral issues—they are the words of revolution, and a revolution seeking nothing less than unconditional surrender from its enemies.

Kaufman went on to argue,

> If the last 50 years . . . have taught us anything, it is that we can indeed bend the arc of the moral universe toward justice. This movement has changed the lives of the LGBTQ community, but it has also changed the way the entire nation thinks and feels about homosexuality, and about the entire spectrum of gender identity and sexual orientation. How can we use what we've learned in those 50 years to combat the current turn toward autocracy?

These words thunder loudly across the moral landscape of Western civilization. The gathering storm rumbles with calls for more revolution. The strides of the gay rights movement over the last half century are not hardly enough to satisfy the revolutionaries. The LGBTQ movement utterly rejected and replaced the ontological realities of gender and sexuality—but it isn't enough. The movement is far more revolutionary than many thought or believed.

Indeed, much of the struggle of the gay rights movement

centered on marriage equality—to legalize same-sex marriage and to enshrine within the moral DNA of America acceptance, celebration, and normalization of same-sex couples in a married union. Despite that vision, the LGBTQ movement cannot keep up with its own radicalizing trends and the trajectory of its own moral reorientation of marriage, sexuality, and gender.

Jeremy Allen wrote an article for the *New York Times* with the headline "Chasing the L.G.B.T.Q. Millennial American Dream: The arrival of marriage equality offers a generation a future they could not have envisioned. But is it what they want?" Throughout his article, Allen chronicles the lack of weddings among gay millennials.[4] Despite the advances of the LGBTQ agenda in American public policy, it turns out that marriage is not the goal for many of the upcoming generation of LGBTQ men and women. Why? Wasn't marriage equality, after all, the hope of the LGBTQ movement and the zenith of its aspirations? Marriage cannot be the answer to this sexual revolution because marriage, as we will see, is still seen by many as a symbol of oppression—a system designed to suppress the sexual liberty championed by the LGBTQ movement. Marriage will not satisfy this revolution because its end result can only be total sexual anarchy. The movement succeeded in convincing the Supreme Court (and millions of Americans) to redefine marriage. But revolutions are never satisfied.

Nathaniel Frank, author of the book *Awakening: How Gays and Lesbians Brought Marriage Equality to America*, wrote an article for the *Washington Post* that also celebrated the fiftieth anniversary of the Stonewall riots. Frank asserted,

> What may seem like a straightforward chance to celebrate progress actually masks a fault line that has divided our movement since its start: whether our goal is equality or liberation, a fight for the right to be treated like everyone else or the freedom to be authentically ourselves. Do we seek belonging in the world as it is

or the chance to transform the world, by throwing off repressive norms, into a place where all of us—queer and non-queer alike—can be more free?[5]

Before Churchill was prime minister, he warned the world of the dangers of Hitler and his Nazi regime. Where many believed that negotiations and diplomacy could secure the avoidance of another global conflict, Churchill knew the folly of such visions of appeasement. The engines of secularization, in the same way, push toward the transformation of the entire culture. Frank stated, "These activists didn't just want to create alternative communities for queer people. They aimed to remake society around the novel social arrangements they cherished: addressing human need and desire through broad community structures rather than monogamous nuclear families." According to Frank, the vision of the LGBTQ movement centered on a comprehensive reorientation of the societal norms that had governed humanity since Adam and Eve.

Frank continued his article, stating, "The LGBT movement, including the push for marriage equality, has also helped upend repressive attitudes about sex, establishing nonmarital sex—and sexual behavior once thought perverse—as largely uncontroversial." This sentence encapsulates the scope of the sexual revolution. Not only did the sexual revolutionaries set out to legalize same-sex marriage; they actually sought a far more fundamental revolution, namely, a comprehensive upending of the entire moral system of sexuality. Indeed, Frank argued, "Stonewall's legacy isn't just about making queer people look more like everyone else. It's also, perhaps more mutinously, about making everyone else look a bit more queer." That is an honest (though audacious) acknowledgment—the goal of the LGBTQ revolutionaries is to make everyone "look a bit more queer." In many sectors of society, they are clearly succeeding.

Transgenderism and the Sexual Revolution

But now, it is abundantly clear that the most radical and revolutionary letter in the LGBTQ anacronym is the "T" for transgender. More than any other component of the LGBTQ revolution, the transgender movement represents an attempt to redefine humanity itself—not just human sexuality. Indeed, many gay and lesbian activists, who ought to celebrate transgenderism, now find themselves on the wrong side of history as the sexual revolution continues to spiral out of their control.

Just consider how the transgender revolution is redefining women and girls' sports and athletic competition. Take Martina Navratilova, for example. She won the Wimbledon women's singles title a phenomenal nine times, but Navratilova's name appears in headlines today not for her athleticism but for her collision with the transgender revolution. Navratilova has long identified as a gay athlete who championed the cause of gay rights. Now, the mainstream of the sexual revolution has disavowed Navratilova for her comments that criticized the participation of transgender women in gender specific sports—that is to say, allowing men who identify as women to compete against actual women in athletic contests.

This controversy began in December 2018 when Navratilova tweeted, "You can't just proclaim yourself a female and be able to compete against women." She advocated for standards that would disqualify biological men from competing against women in athletic events.

Navratilova faced immediate backlash from the transgender community. Activists lambasted Navratilova and warned her that she was about to be on the wrong side of history. Once a leader and international symbol of the gay rights revolution, Navratilova had been left behind—her views were no longer in step with the sweeping moral upheaval propagated by the sexual revolutionaries. After the backlash, Navratilova deleted her tweet and promised to study the issue in depth.

That was late 2018. Then, in February 2019, the *Sunday Times* published Navratilova's expanded argument in an article with the headline "The Rules on Trans Athletes Reward Cheats and Punish the Innocent."[6]

Navratilova began her article, writing, "Shortly before Christmas I inadvertently stumbled into the mother and father of a spat about gender and fair play in sport. It began with an instinctive reaction and a tweet that I wrote on a serious forum dealing with the subject. . . . Perhaps I could have phrased it more delicately and less dogmatically, but I was not prepared for the onslaught that followed."

She described how she did what any rational person would do when presented with a moral quandary: she decided to learn about the subject she had addressed in her tweet and allowed herself time for contemplation on this important issue. After her time of reflection, she came to the same conclusion—when sports organizations capitulate to the trans-agenda and allow transgender women to compete against other women, they foster an environment of cheating.

Navratilova made her arguments based on the nature of hormones and biology. She stated,

If anything, my views have strengthened. To put the argument at its most basic: a man can decide to be female, take hormones if required by whatever sporting organization is concerned, win everything in sight and perhaps earn a small fortune, and then reverse his decision and go back to making babies if he so desires. It's insane and it's cheating. I am happy to address a transgender woman in whatever form she prefers, but I would not be happy to compete against her. It would not be fair. Simply reducing hormone levels—the prescription most sports have adopted—does not solve the problem. A man builds up muscle and bone density, as well as a greater number of oxygen-carrying red blood cells, from childhood. Training increases the discrepancy. Indeed, if a male were to change gender in such a way as to eliminate any accumulated advantage, he would have to begin hormone treatment before puberty. For me, that is unthinkable.

What is unthinkable for Navratilova is exactly the direction of the transgender revolutionaries—they actively advocate the use of puberty-blocking hormone treatments and allowing children and teenagers to "transition." The dizzying speed of the sexual revolution blazed ahead of Navratilova, leaving her behind in its redefinition of reality.

Navratilova's argument is quite simple: a transgender woman, rightly understood, is not a woman. A transgender woman, regardless of self-conscious identity or feeling, does not possess the biological structure of a female body. This is true even after so-called gender reassignment surgery. This presents an unfair advantage for transgender women who, despite hormone treatments, still possess at least some of the physical qualities and attributes of a male body. A female transgender athlete benefits from the bone density, muscle mass, skeletal structure, and circulatory system of a man, even if hormones are adjusted. According to Navratilova, hundreds of trans-athletes, specifically transgender women, ride the waves of the moral revolution into the realm of competitive sports and, through their unfair advantage, win sporting contests against women.

As Navratilova stood her ground, the backlash from the moral revolutionaries only increased. The transgender elites unseated Navratilova as a spokesperson for gay rights. This new development marks a collision between traditional gay rights activists and the new transgender activists. Navratilova finds herself caught in the chaos of the moral revolution as the winds have now turned against her and her outdated, antiquated gay rights morality. This story is not about the secular worldview colliding with a biblical worldview, but a collision within the secularist mindset itself. The moral revolution leads to a confusion in which the new activists turn on the old activists, because people like Navratilova are not pressing the new agenda far enough.

This collision sparks controversy in every sphere of public life. For example, historic women's colleges, which hold to a radical feminist ideology, now find themselves on the wrong side of their own history as the earthquakes of the sexual revolution reach their campuses. The LGBTQ agenda takes the objective distinctions "male" and "female" and reorients it around subjective, individual experience and identity. This presents an enormous problem even for liberal, feminist women's schools who receive applications for admission from transgender women. Make no mistake, you cannot remain a historic women's college and join the transgender revolution, but most of these historic colleges are trying to live the contradiction. They insist that they remain for women only, but openly accept biological males as students.

This is a complete meltdown of moral order, and this is exactly what the revolutionaries have set loose. The headlines will continue down this trend—we will see not only liberals versus conservatives but revolutionaries versus revolutionaries; feminist ideology versus transgender ideology; gay and lesbian activism against transgender activism. This recent controversy surrounding Martina Navratilova shows the utter inconsistencies inherent in the sexual revolution's ideology.

Martina Navratilova once served as an activist and intellectual symbol for the gay rights movement. Now, the moral revolution has run right past her and declared her the problem. That's the way radical revolutions work. They eventually turn on their own.

Indeed, the transgender movement revved at such swiftness that even the engines of the sexual revolution and the secular elites cannot keep up with its chaos. During the tumultuous 1970s, comedienne Lily Tomlin famously quipped, "I'm trying to be cynical, but it's hard to keep up." It seems as if her lament of the speed of the times applies to our current moment, which is caught amid the torrent of the sexual revolution and the dominance of transgenderism on the sexual revolution. Who *can* keep up?

Two articles from the *New York Times* illustrate the quandary of even a secular paper trying to keep up the pace with the transgender movement. Amy Harmon wrote the first article with the headline "Which Box Do You Check? Some States Are Offering a Nonbinary Option."[7] Harmon wrote, "As nonbinary teenagers push for driver's licenses that reflect their identity, a fraught debate over the nature of gender has arrived in the nation's statehouses."

Harmon begins the article, writing,

> Ever since El Martinez started asking to be called by the gender-neutral pronouns "they/them" in the ninth grade, they have fielded skepticism in a variety of forms and from a multitude of sources about what it means to identify as nonbinary. There are faculty advisers on El's theater crew who balk at using "they" for one person; classmates at El's public school on the outskirts of Boston who insist El can't be "multiple people"; and commenters on El's social media feeds who dismiss nonbinary gender identities like androgyne (a combination of masculine and feminine), agender (the absence of gender) and gender-fluid (moving between genders) as lacking a basis in biology.

Just two paragraphs into the article and we have witnessed the absolute breakdown in language. We now live in a world advocating for the use of "they/them" to refer to one person. Indeed, as the article records, the Massachusetts legislature considered a bill that would add an "X" option for nonbinary genders on a driver's license. The bill, however, was shelved after a Republican representative proposed an amendment, which mandated that the state offer twenty-nine other gender options that would include pangender, two-spirit, and genderqueer.

Harmon wrote, "Rather than open the requisite debate on each term, leaders of the Democratic-controlled House shelved the measure."

Here is the sad tale of the sexual revolution's consequences on a society. We once thought that transgender meant a person who was born anatomically male or female but wanted to present themselves and be considered as the opposite gender.

We thought that's what it meant. How wrong we were.

It turns out that the transgender activists demand far more than perhaps even the earlier sexual revolutionaries could have imagined. Indeed, Ev Even, the director of the Massachusetts Transgender Political Coalition, said in the article, "He [the Republican representative] articulated an anxiety that many people, even folks from the left, have: that there's this slippery slope of identity, and 'Where will it stop?'"

If the left is now asking this question, we face a moral revolution out of control.

Later in the article, Harmon wrote, "For their part, some non-binary people suggest that concerns about authenticity and grammar sidestep thornier questions about the culture's longstanding limits on how gender is supposed to be felt and expressed."

Here, the transgender activists demand society overcome the antiquated, outmoded labels like "male" and "female"—these represent oppressive vestiges of a bygone era, namely, all of human history.

The *New York Times* goes on to report,

The wave of proposed gender-neutral legislation has prompted debate over whether extending legal recognition to a category of people still unknown to many Americans could undermine support for other groups vulnerable to discrimination. It has also highlighted how disorienting it can be to lose the gendered cues, like pronouns, names, appearance, and mannerisms, that shape so much of social interaction.

Whether Harmon intended to or not, in this quote she acknowledged that our entire social ordering and our civilization require a basic ability to say, "That's a man," and "That's a woman."

Our society charged forward under the banner of the sexual revolution. Now, some of its adherents are realizing that this really isn't going to work. Indeed, this article highlights the collision of the sexual revolution with other cherished, liberal movements like feminism. If being female is not grounded in biology, but is relegated to subjectivism and the internal mind, then you cannot have feminism. The *New York Times* cites a leader with the Women's Liberation Front who stated, "To deny the reality of sex means we're not able to name, address, and fix systemic sex-based oppression and exploitation."

But the transgender revolutionaries explicitly attempt to dismantle the binary realities of gender. The article quotes an advocate for a gender-neutral license bill, stating, "The gender binary is a system of control that a lot of nonbinary people are invested in destroying, and this is a step toward that."

We can at least be thankful for the candor of the sexual revolutionaries. They know they call for mutiny; they know they summon society to depart from oppressive cultural constructs like gender—not only must divergent ideologies surrender, they must be destroyed.

Only a few days after Harmon's article ran, the *New York Times* published another story by Daniel Bergner with the headline "The Struggles of Rejecting the Gender Binary." Bergner wrote, "Not everyone identifies as male or female. This is what it's like to be nonbinary in a world that wants to box you in."[8]

This is a massive article with enormous worldview implications, readily apparent in the obfuscated gender language of the transgender revolution. The article begins by telling us about an individual who had been born male and began to identify as female and who concluded he should transition to a female gender identity and rename himself Hannah.

In the process of following what was revolutionary just a couple of years ago, this individual discovered that, according to his own self-understanding, he is actually neither a man nor a woman. This individual now believes he has a gender-nonbinary identity. He has left his male name, his chosen female name, and instead adopted the nonbinary name Salem. He also wants to be referred to by the supposed gender-neutral pronouns "they/them." The article states,

> They'd failed, so far, to get their parents, their sister, or their two remaining friends to understand and accept that they were neither a man nor a woman, that they were nonbinary, gender fluid, gender expansive. They'd chosen the name Salem to fit with their identity, but they'd almost never asked anyone to call them by it. It was easier—definitely not easy, but easier—to let themselves be considered conventionally transgender male to female, and go by the name Hannah.

The English language cannot bear this. Throughout the article, there are at least 170 cases where the pronoun "he" or "she" should be used. Instead, the transgender revolution has adopted a vocabulary of confusion and chaos. But Christians understand that something far more troubling lies behind the breakdown of language—something more fundamental. Truth itself has been subverted.

The gender revolutionaries have set a trap for themselves. They have said that individual autonomy is the ultimate source of meaning when it comes to sexuality, marriage, relationships, gender, personal identity, you name it. And if individual autonomy is the only determining issue, then every individual gets to be autonomous and categories such as male and female or even LGBTQ are out the window.

Instead, we have an endless permutation. Even in this article we read, "An abundance of labels with subtle distinctions are in play.

Neutrois and gender nonconforming and demiboy and demigirl and pangender and genderqueer are among the array of closely related identities that could confound any demographer."

The revolution itself cannot keep up with its own consequences. When the transgender movement jettisoned objective truth and reality, they opened the door to a dizzying array of flux, autonomous gender-labels; and new labels appear about every fifteen minutes. No one can keep up. No one can keep count—not even the revolutionaries.

This article from the *New York Times* makes every attempt to deploy the transgender language and terminology consistently and coherently. But hard as the paper tries, the article breaks down and the reader cannot make sense of who or what is being referenced. Coherence breaks down because the transgender worldview is itself incoherent. It has abandoned both coherence and consistency. It denies the goodness of the created order. It has exchanged the truth about God for a lie and has chosen instead to worship the creature rather than the Creator.

Christians reading this article must be heartbroken. Why? Because the transgender movement has made promises it cannot keep. The article chronicles the story of Kai, another individual like Salem. Bergner retells his interview with Kai, writing,

> Logically and philosophically, for Kai, bodies signified nothing; physiology was without meaning. "But I do—I care, very much," he said. Logic and longing were irreconcilable. And for someone as smart and scientific as Kai, this was barely endurable. The contradiction between anatomical irrelevance and anatomical yearning was an existential challenge. "What I'm feeling is that there's this internal, eternal thing that is always going to be saying, 'You as you exist are not real.'"

This line of reasoning shows that the transgender movement offers false and dangerous promises. It is looking for freedom in all the wrong places. It is offering all the wrong answers to life's most important questions. Transgenderism writes checks that bounce. It offers a lie veiled in truth and happiness. It will only end in more brokenness and pain, devastation and destruction.

Despite the inherent failure and brokenness of the transgender promise, the movement presses toward new initiatives like a moth to a flame. The *New York Times* article tells about the author of a book entitled *You're in the Wrong Bathroom.* The author is identified as "something of a visionary outlining a future when technology that's already near—sensate prostheses; virtual reality that's thoroughly immersive—will make our relationships to our bodies 'artistic, the results of acts of creation.'"

That last sentence actually continues, using language that ought not to be repeated. Notwithstanding, the important line is that our new gender identity will be an act of our own creation. We will create ourselves. But creation implies a creator. Who is the real creator? For the transgender movement, the creator is the autonomous individual. We have seen this idea before. In Genesis 3, Adam and Eve rebelled against their Creator and thought they themselves could be like God. The transgender movement recapitulates the very sin committed in Eden. Try as they may, the transgender movement cannot escape *the Creator.* In the end, we cannot create ourselves.

Some will still try, however. The *New York Times* makes clear that the transgender activists are "foreseeing a time when people passing each other on the street wouldn't immediately, unconsciously sort one another into male or female." Then, the Bergner article quotes Laura Jacobs, a nonbinary therapist who stated, "I don't know what genders are going to look like four generations from now. I think we're going to perceive each other as people. The classifications we live under will fall by the wayside." This is not a morally passive statement—it amounts to an all-out repudiation of the biblical worldview, the dignity of maleness and femaleness, and anything resembling a sane, sexual ethic.

The Revolution's Demand to the Church of Jesus Christ

The secular age can only sow greater confusion on issues of gender and sexuality. Though the United States and other Western nations were not "Christian" in the sense that everyone was a believing Christian, they were at least governed by a biblical worldview that upheld the dignity of gender and sexuality. That worldview has now been displaced, and a new sexual ethic governed by the LGBTQ movement has replaced the biblical vision of gender and sexuality. The stability and communal understandings central to social cohesion are now undermined, often by the coercive power of the state apparatus. This much is clear: when societies reject the natural, creational order that God put in place, chaos and confusion follow.

This new phase of revolution, however, assaults not only the pillars of Western civilization, but the church of Jesus Christ. Indeed, in this secular moment, Christians face enormous pressure to the revolution; and this revolution demands unilateral surrender. It is the Christian worldview that uniquely infuriates the new revolutionaries, for it is the biblical categories of personhood that shaped the societies of Europe and North America. Sadly, many churches have capitulated to the demands of the sexual revolution. It will take extraordinary conviction to resist their revolution. We are about to find out which churches, denominations, and Christian institutions are capable of this resistance. The church has never faced a challenge quite like this.

The sexual revolution requires a total redefining of morality, cultural authority, personal identity, and more. The revolution requires a new vocabulary and a radically revised dictionary. Ultimately, the moral revolutionaries seek to redefine reality itself. And this revolution has no stopping point. The plus sign at the end of LGBTQ+ is a signal of more challenges sure to come.

We must pay close attention to renewed efforts to redefine and recast the evangelical concept of sexuality and gender. Evangelicalism does not hold to a distinctively evangelical view of sexual morality and personal identity. Instead, evangelical Christians have maintained the framework of morality, marriage, and gender that has been common to all Christians throughout time. The evangelical distinctive is to hold these convictions based on the authority of Scripture, not merely because their convictions are deeply ingrained in the tradition of the church. But, as it turns out, evangelicals may stand virtually alone in affirming and teaching what the Christian church has taught for two thousand years.

For this reason, we must look very carefully at any attempt to reshape how evangelicals think about these issues. A clear challenge came in the form of the 2018 Revoice Conference. Revoice was advertised as "supporting, encouraging, and empowering gay, lesbian, same sex-attracted, and other LGBT Christians so they can flourish while observing the historic, Christian doctrine of marriage and sexuality."[9] On the surface, this seems like a positive statement. Indeed, it is encouraging to hear of Christians who seek the flourishing of their brothers and sisters in Christ who struggle with same-sex attraction by helping them live within the historic affirmations of Christian orthodoxy. The devil, however, is in the details.

The name was no accident, as the organizers called for a "revoicing" of the evangelical message on issues of sexuality, sexual identity, and beyond.

The organizers stated plainly that they,

Envision a future Christianity where LGBT people can be open and transparent in their faith communities about their orientation and/or experience of gender dysphoria without feeling inferior to their straight, cisgender brothers and sisters; where churches not only utilize but also celebrate the unique opportunities that life-long celibate LGBT people have to serve others; where Christian leaders boast about the faith of LGBT people who are living a sacrificial obedience for the sake of the Kingdom; and where LGBT people are welcomed into families so they, too, can experience the joys, challenges, and benefits of kinship.[10]

They also stated emphatically:

We believe that the Bible restricts sexual activity to the context of a marriage covenant, which is defined in the Bible as the emotional, spiritual, and physical union of a man and a woman that is ordered toward procreation. At the same time, we also believe that the Bible honors those who live out an extended commitment to celibacy, and that unmarried people should play a uniquely valuable role in the lives of local faith communities.[11]

They acknowledged that these convictions "constitute the 'traditional sexual ethic,' because it represents the worldview that the Bible consistently teaches across both the Old and New Testaments and that Christians have historically believed for millennia."

In other contexts, organizers have identified themselves with "great tradition Christianity," a recognition of a constant pattern of Christian teaching faithful to Scripture. That theological tradition is the source of the "traditional sexual ethic" acknowledged by the organizers. The language is important, as language always is. The mission statement and website of the conference refer over and over again to "LGBT people" and uses the language of "sexual minorities" and even "queer Christians."

The principal organizer of the conference, Nate Collins, told *Christianity Today*: "We all believe that the Bible teaches a traditional, historic understanding of sexuality in marriage, and so we are not attempting in any way to redefine any of those doctrines. We're trying to live within the bounds of historic Christian teaching about sexuality and gender. But we find difficulty doing that for a lot of reasons."[12]

Actually, the signals sent by many involved in the conference are a bit confusing, to say the least. In recent years, some in the evangelical world have proposed the categories of "Side A" and "Side B" Christians who identify as LGBTQ. Side A refers to those who have abandoned the historic Christian teaching about sexuality and marriage and now affirm same-sex relationships and same-sex marriage. The Side A advocates are associated more with liberal Protestant denominations that long ago abandoned biblical orthodoxy and now preach the sexual revolution.

Side B refers to those who identify as both LGBTQ and Christian, and who affirm the traditional Christian ethic on sexuality and marriage. Revoice seems clearly to identify as Side B, but some of the main organizers and speakers gladly join in common efforts with Side A advocates. LGBTQ identity binds Side A and Side B advocates together.

We should also note that Revoice did not have much of a voice on transgender questions. It is not at all clear, for example, what in the leaders' minds celibacy or a commitment to "the historic Christian doctrine of marriage and sexuality" is supposed to mean for the "T" in LGBT. Even the use of "LGBT" in this context is impossible to square with "historic Christian teaching about sexuality and gender."

Gregory Coles, author of *Single, Gay, Christian*, was a worship leader for Revoice. In the book, Coles raises the scenario of two women who identify as Christians, one a lesbian married to a woman and the other a "straight" Christian who says she believes in the biblical ethic restricting sex to marriage between a man and a woman, but who is promiscuous in a series of heterosexual relationships. Coles then wrote, "Theologically, I am more in agreement with the second friend. But whose life is most honoring to God? Who really loves Jesus more? Who am I more likely to see in heaven? I don't know."[13]

Of course, that is a strange and forced scenario. The biblical answer would be that both women are living in sinful violation of Scripture.

Earlier in the book, Coles spoke of being in a room that included some who identify as Side A and some who identify as Side B (as Coles does). But his description of the predicament is telling. When asked to identify as Side A or Side B, Coles wrote: "I didn't want to be reduced to a simple yes or no. I wanted a new side, something further along the alphabet, something full of asterisks and footnotes and caveats. I've never been fluent in the language of binaries."

Several issues press for immediate attention. One is the identification of people as "LGBT Christians" or "gay Christians." This language implies that Christians can be identified in an ongoing manner with a sexual identity that is contrary to Scripture. Behind the language is the modern conception of identity theory that is, in the end, fundamentally unbiblical. The use of the language of "sexual minorities" is a further extension of identity theory and modern critical theory and analysis. In this context, "sexual minority" simultaneously implies permanent identity and a demand for recognition as a minority. As pastor and author Kevin DeYoung rightly noted, the use of this language implies a political status.

The larger problem is the idea that any believer can claim identity with a pattern of sexual attraction that is itself sinful. The apostle Paul answered this question definitively when he explained in 1 Corinthians 6:11, "Such were some of you. But you were washed, you were sanctified, you were justified in the name of the Lord Jesus Christ and the Spirit of our God."

There have been Christian believers throughout the entire history of the church who have struggled with same-sex temptation and who have come to know that pattern of temptation as what we now understand as a sexual orientation. In his book *All But Invisible*, Nate Collins argued that the most important element in same-sex orientation is its "givenness." By that he means that it is an orientation or pattern of attraction that is not chosen but discovered.

But "givenness" in a fallen world does not mean that the orientation—the same-sex attraction itself—is not sinful. The Bible identifies internal temptation as sin (James 1:14). Denny Burk and Heath Lambert argue that "same-sex attraction, not just homosexual behavior, is sinful."[14] We are called to repent both of sin and of any inner temptation to sin.

The issues here are bigger than sexuality. As Denny Burk and Rosaria Butterfield rightly explain, we confront here a basic evangelical disagreement with Roman Catholicism.[15] Ever since the Council of Trent (1545–1563), the Roman Catholic Church has insisted that involuntary incentive to sin is not itself sin. In the most amazing sentence, the Council of Trent declared: "This concupiscence, which the apostle sometimes calls sin, the holy Synod declares that the Catholic Church has never understood it to be called sin." Don't miss the acknowledgment that the doctrine of Trent is contrary to the language of the apostle.

John Calvin referred to concupiscence as "depraved" and "at variance with rectitude." In this verdict, Calvin was joined by other Protestants—and the New Testament. Just think of the language of the historic *Book of Common Prayer*, praying in repentance for the "devices and desires of our own hearts."

Surely, the mortification of sin required of Christians would demand that we put as much distance as possible between ourselves and any temptation to sin (Rom. 8:12–13).

In the interview with *Christianity Today* just prior to the conference, Nate Collins attempted to respond to criticisms by insisting, as he does in his book, that sexual orientation and same-sex attraction are not always erotic but can be celebrated as aesthetic and relational. He affirms that same-sex sexual attraction is sinful, but he argues that sexual orientation is actually not necessarily erotic but centered in "the perception and admiration of personal beauty."

In his book he refers to this as an "aesthetic orientation," a term he concedes is his own.

Wesley Hill, another speaker at Revoice, is a major proponent of "spiritual friendships" within LGBTQ identity. He has written: "Being gay is, for me, as much a sensibility as anything else: a heightened sensitivity to and passion for same-sex beauty."[16]

Same-sex attraction is not limited to sexual attraction, but it strains all credibility to argue that this "aesthetic orientation" can be nonsexual. Considered more closely, the "aesthetic orientation" actually appears to be even more deeply rooted in a sinful impulse. Aesthetic attractions are as corrupted by sin as the sexual passions. To put the matter bluntly, are we to affirm that an "aesthetic orientation" toward the same sex is pure and blameless and nonsexual? This would be severe pastoral malpractice.

Speakers at Revoice pointed to Ruth and Naomi, and David and Jonathan, as biblical examples, but in both cases the relationship was clearly and definitively neither erotic nor aesthetic and references to them in this light are deliberately misleading. The "spiritual friendship" model, related to LGBTQ identity, is just not compatible with an evangelical biblical theology, even if Catholics can eagerly affirm the idea.

In one of the more astounding moments of Revoice, Nate Collins read from Jeremiah 15 and then asked:

Is it possible that gay people today are being sent by God, like Jeremiah, to find God's words for the church, to eat them and make them our own? To shed light on contemporary false teachings and even idolatries, not just the false teaching of the progressive sexual ethic, but other more subtle forms of false teaching? Is it possible that gender and sexual minorities who have lived lives of costly obedience are themselves a prophetic call to the church to abandon idolatrous attitudes toward the nuclear family, toward sexual pleasure? If so, we are prophets.

Idolatry of the nuclear family? Here we see the destabilizing power of the sexual revolution and modern critical theory at full force—but now from inside the walls of Christianity.

It is, of course, possible for human beings to idolize anything, but that is not what is really at stake in Collins's comment. He really claims that gay people are called to a prophetic role to correct the church for believing in the normative nature of the nuclear family.

Before pressing further, we should note that the term "nuclear family," referring to a father and mother and their children in one household, is a fairly recent term, dating back only to the twentieth century. The family, of course, is as old as Genesis. The more accurate term for describing the family is not nuclear but natural or conjugal.

And right there is the issue. What the Bible reveals, from Genesis 1 onward, is the fact that God created human beings as male and female, both made in his image, and made for the conjugal relationship of marriage and procreation, which is the very first divine command to humankind (Gen. 1:28). Marriage, the conjugal union of a man and a woman, is revealed as God's creative purpose, from the beginning.

Even those men and women who do not marry are defined by the conjugal union that brought them into being and by the normative nature of the natural family (both "nuclear" and extended) that is honored throughout holy Scripture. The subversion of marriage and the family has been one of the most devastating results of modernity, and this very subversion is central to the ambitions of the sexual revolutionaries. Now, this revolution seeks the utter destruction of historic Christianity.

In his book, Collins identified "heteronormativity" as a central problem in both secular society and the church: "It's one thing to say that the only kind of sexual expression permitted by Scripture is the heterosexual pattern. It's another thing to say that heterosexual orientations as they are embedded in our fallen world are not sinful in themselves because they match the general creational pattern."[17]

That is simply wrong. Every human being past puberty is a sexual sinner of some form, but the attraction of a man to a woman, completed in the conjugal union of marriage, is precisely "the general creational pattern." Furthermore, in Romans 1:26–27 the apostle Paul referred to same-sex passion and activity as "contrary to nature"—thus the rejection of the "general creational pattern."

After the fall, all human beings are born sinners and fall short of both the glory of God and the clear testimony of creation (Rom. 3:23; 1:18–32), but the creational pattern itself is not sinful. The New Testament presents the church as the family of faith, made up of all those adopted by God through Christ. Thus, all believers are brothers and sisters in one household of faith. Furthermore, the New Testament explicitly honors celibacy (which by the way, only makes sense against the background of normative marriage and family life), but that celibacy is chaste in form and directed toward gospel deployment (1 Cor. 7:1–8). Collins rightly calls on congregations to leave no member without inclusion in family life—a searing indictment of many congregations, to be sure. Similarly, Rosaria Butterfield has underlined the priority of gospel hospitality among Christians.

But denouncing "idolatrous attitudes toward the nuclear family" as a claimed prophetic role for those who identify as LGBTQ+ Christians reveals just how far the ideology of the sexual revisionists has reached even within American Christianity. The relativizing of the natural conjugal family represents what English journalist and satirist Malcolm Muggeridge called the "great liberal death wish." It stands in direct contradiction to the mandate given by God in Genesis 1:28. The Great Commission expands that mandate; it does not reverse it.

Even before the Revoice Conference began, notice was given of a session entitled "Redeeming Queer Culture: An Adventure." The description is itself astounding:

> For the sexual minority seeking to submit his or her life fully to Christ and to the historic Christian sexual ethic, queer culture presents a bit of a dilemma; rather than combing through and analyzing which parts are to be rejected, or redeemed, or to be received with joy (Acts 17:16–34), Christians have often discarded the virtues of queer culture along with the vices, which leaves culturally connected Christian sexual minorities torn between two cultures, two histories, and two communities. So questions that have until now been largely unanswered remain: what does queer culture (and specifically, queer literature and theory) have to offer us who follow Christ? What queer treasure, honor, and glory will be brought into the New Jerusalem at the end of time (Revelation 21:24–26)?

Putting the pieces together, it becomes clear that Revoice and its organizers would rewrite the meta-narrative of Scripture so that Creation before the fall is not heterosexual in orientation and can even include same-sex "aesthetic orientation." The fall is limited in its extent to our sin nature; redemption does not mean that the "new creature" in Christ will break from identity with sin, and the New Creation will include "treasure, honor, and glory" from queer culture.

There is another big issue embedded in that session description. Note the mention of "culturally connected Christian sexual minorities." At first glance, that might seem to mean something like a connection to the culture at large. But in the language of the LGBTQ+ community, it means connection to "queer culture." The "culturally connected Christian sexual minority" (watch every word carefully) is, as the statement emphasizes, "torn between two cultures, two histories, and two communities." That means torn between queer culture and the church.

That, to state the matter clearly, is unstable, unfaithful, unworkable, unbiblical, indeed, impossible.

This returns us to the issue of sexual identity and Christian identity once again. A Christian who identifies as LGBTQ+ will certainly pray for and be concerned for the conversion of friends in the LGBTQ+ community, and we can pray that personal friendships and Christian hospitality can lead to gospel advance among these friends and the LGBTQ+ community. But the identity of a Christian cannot be with any culture defined in its essence by the rejection of God's design and command. Though that language has received scant attention, it is among the most important associated with Revoice.

And the issue of language arises again and again and again. In his main address to the conference, Nate Collins lamented: "I'm tired. I'm tired of people saying I'm using the wrong words. I'm tired of people saying I'm not using enough of the right words."

In his interview with *Christianity Today*, Collins conceded that some of the language used on the website for the conference was seen as revealing a "slippery slope ethically," but he defended even the language by saying: "Right now the conversation on LGBT issues and gender, sexuality, and evangelicalism is fragmented. There's a lot of groups of people that use language in very specific ways that makes sense to them but doesn't make sense to people outside of their tribe."

Later, Collins said: "We're just trying to make space for people for whom the language they use is meaningful, in terms of how they are trying to reconcile their gender and sexuality with their faith."

At one very strange level, that is an open admission that the self-expressive language of many in the Revoice community reflects a movement in flux and in motion, even in language.

But references to "queer culture" are not accidental, and the language from the conference is clear enough. Revoice represents an attempt to build a halfway house between LGBTQ+ culture and evangelical Christianity. They want to define what they mean by "Side B," when the LGBTQ+ culture is unambiguously "Side A."

We should take the organizers of Revoice at their word and hear what they are saying. We should lament the brokenness and understand the many failings of the Christian church toward those who identify with the LGBTQ+ community. But we dare not add yet another failure to those failures. We cannot see Revoice as anything other than a house built upon the sand. Revoice is not the voice of faithful Christianity.

Faithfulness Amid the Storm

Why not just join the revolution? This question seems obvious to many people who look at conservative Christians and honestly wonder why we cannot just change our views on homosexuality, same-sex marriage, and the entire LGBTQ constellation of issues. We are constantly told that we must abandon the clear teachings of the Bible in order to get "on the right side of history." It's not that we don't understand the argument—we simply do not accept it.

Christians today not only face the aftermath of this revolution, but are presented daily with horrifyingly new challenges amid a storm that seeks to destroy any semblance of our creational identity—the glorious reality of being man and woman created in the *imago Dei*, the very image of God. The challenges the church faces multiply day by day and increase in complexity and danger. Notwithstanding, the church of Jesus Christ must stand and meet this storm of secularism with the full force of the gospel. The stakes are too grave. The fight too important. We cannot be silent—we cannot surrender.

Clearly, many more liberal churches and denominations are not only accepting the LGBTQ argument, they are running away with it. Each of these churches once defined marriage exclusively as the union of a man and a woman, and every one of them once defined human sexuality and gender in agreement with the Bible and with historic Christian teachings. Church after church, denomination after denomination, however, has capitulated to the sexual revolutionaries. In the name of cultural relevance or doctrinal ambivalence, many believe the historic theological commitments of the church to be misguided and to belong to the annals of antiquity. Now, at least some people seem genuinely perplexed that conservative Christians will not just go along with the program to redefine Christian morality, marriage, and doctrine.

The biblical worldview, however, leaves no room for capitulation nor any room for surrender. The theological issues that surround gender and sexuality are not subsidiary questions—the questions surrounding gender and sexuality gravitate around our very identity as human beings and our view of the character of God. We will not surrender because we cannot. Unlike those who embrace liberal theology, we do not see Christianity as a system of beliefs that we can just change as we see fit. We do not see the Bible as a mere collection of ancient religious writings that can be disregarded or reinterpreted to mean something other than what it says.

Instead, we understand the Bible to be what it claims to be, nothing less than the inspired and inerrant Word of God. We understand Christianity to be grounded in specific truths as revealed by Christ and the apostles and given to us in the holy Scriptures. We believe that Christianity is defined by what the Bible calls "the faith that was once for all delivered to the saints" (Jude v. 3).

These days, we find ourselves opposed, dismissed, and ridiculed for holding to truths that the Christian church has taught for two thousand years.

Indeed, as noted earlier, the battle that rages is between *revolution* and *revelation*. This is why the church cannot recede or diminish its commitments on gender and sexuality. Either we engage in active revolution against God, or we hold fast to the verbal revelation God granted us in his Word and in Jesus Christ. The sexual revolution—now undermining the very structure of humanity as male and female—represents a direct challenge to what Christians believe and teach and preach. The LGBTQ revolution is just the latest representation of the perennial human temptation to reject God's creational ordinances and humanity's identity and purpose. But it will not lead to human flourishing nor happiness—it cannot. Fundamental to the Christian worldview is the truth that our identity can only be established by the Creator—and we can only be rescued from ourselves and from our sin by the Redeemer.

The reality is that Christians who define Christianity in terms of historic Christian doctrine and moral teachings do not believe merely that these teachings are true, but that they point to the only truth that will produce real and lasting human happiness. We are not merely opposed to same-sex marriage because we believe it to be contrary to Scripture; we believe that anything opposed to Scripture cannot lead to human flourishing.

There can be no question that we are living in the midst of a vast revolution in moral values. The more liberal churches and denominations can simply accommodate themselves to this moral revolution and move on. But in so doing they are abandoning not only the clear teachings of the Bible but also the essence of the gospel of Jesus Christ.

That good news promises salvation to anyone who believes in Christ as the crucified and resurrected Lord and who repents of sin. If we misunderstand or misrepresent what sin is, we undercut the work of Christ and our knowledge of the fact that we need a Savior. Furthermore, if we abandon the teachings of the Bible on sexual morality, we confuse the world—and ourselves—about repentance.

The Bible is not merely an inspired book of doctrinal truths. It tells a story of God's act of creation and of the reality of human sin, of the depth of God's saving love for us in Christ, and the story of where history is headed. The Bible also warns us against any effort to change that story or to tell it wrongly. Yes, it warns us against the sin of teaching what the Bible calls "another gospel" than the gospel of Jesus Christ.

The current American landscape includes more liberal churches that are doing their best to join the sexual revolution and conservative churches that cannot follow. Simple honesty requires acknowledgment that it is the conservative churches that are teaching what Christianity has taught for two millennia. We are told that holding to biblical authority and the historic Christian faith will lead to our marginalization.

Perhaps so, but it is the more liberal churches that have been hemorrhaging members by the millions for the last four decades and, even in a secularizing age, it is the most secularized denominations that have suffered the greatest membership losses.

We do understand what is at stake in terms of the human judgment of history. Indeed, the current political crisis reveals much of the trajectory of American public opinion. Day after day, minute by minute, an increasingly secularized American landscape demands that churches and denominations make accommodations to the sexual revolution—to refuse is tantamount, says the culture, to enacting the same level of discrimination exercised by slaveholders and proponents of Jim Crow. This current election cycle highlights, in so many ways, the speed of this sexual revolution and the extent to which candidates and party platforms will bow to this radical moral agenda.

Christians, however, are far more concerned about the divine verdict of eternity. Being on the right side of history is indeed important—but that history must be in line with the trajectory of the cosmos, namely, a day of judgment with Jesus Christ on the judgment seat. This is a comfort to the faithful who hold fast but devastation to those who bow to the gods of secularism. Biblical

Christianity must speak the truth in love and seek to be good neighbors to all, but we cannot abandon the faith just because we are told that we are now on the wrong side of history.

Christians and the church must, therefore, hold fast to revelation and never step off the rock of God's perfect Word. When faced with unprecedented challenges, when secularization makes its harrowing demands, when all chaos breaks loose and society plummets down a spiral of destruction, the church must stand ready with the Bible—the perfect, never-failing, infallible revelation from God. What else will be our authority?

In response to the storm gathering over gender and sexuality, Christians must do at least two things: preach true gospel liberty in the face of erotic liberty and stand ready to receive the refugees of the sexual revolution.

Individual autonomy drives the sexual revolution. The sexual revolutionaries seek liberation from oppressive systems of morality that govern sexual expression. The biblical ethic, in the eyes of this revolution, represents an outdated overlord, seeking nothing but control over the individual. Once overthrown, individuals can express their sexuality without the shackles of an outmoded, backward sexual ethic.

There is a tragic irony embedded within this mindset, and Christians ought to be the ones to cast a spotlight on this immensely flawed and deadly logic. In the pursuit of individual liberty, the outcome is continued bondage—bondage to whatever might be the prevailing cultural ethic. True liberation comes only through the gospel of Jesus Christ. The apostle Paul wrote in Galatians 5:1, "For freedom Christ has set us free; stand firm therefore, and do not submit again to a yoke of slavery."

The sexual revolution aims at liberation. But its promise is false and its "truths" are always changing. The church must hold fast to what the esteemed twentieth-century Welsh preacher Martyn Lloyd-Jones called "truth unchanged and unchanging." That is just about the most countercultural message we might imagine. The gospel reminds us that only through Christ can we experience the power of God's love. Only through the cross can we be transferred from the kingdom of darkness and into the kingdom of eternal light.

This reality leads to the second thing Christians must do in the wake of the sexual rebellion—we must be ready to receive its refugees. We know that the sexual revolution cannot fulfill its promises. The moral revolutionaries embarked on a propaganda campaign, promising fulfillment and acceptance. This is especially true in the transgender movement, where many men and women—and increasingly young boys and girls—even undergo a "gender reassignment" surgery. Through hormone treatments and surgeries, the transgender revolution promises its followers a life of fulfillment and a new identity. Many now regret their decision. We are doomed if we believe that our identity can be recovered by surgery or therapy. In the end, only the God who made us in the beginning can give us an authentic identity.

This revolution will leave in its wake refugees hurt and let down—indeed, even worse. The church of Jesus Christ must be ready to receive them with grace, love, and tender compassion. Jesus designed his ministry around being with sinners—he ate with them, loved them, and went into their homes, often to the dismay of the religious elites. In Luke 19:10, Jesus declared, "For the Son of Man came to seek and to save the lost." Regrettably, the church has often ostracized many in the LGBTQ community through harmful rhetoric and a self-rightousness that is unbecoming of Christ's church. The people of God serve as the embassy of God to a lost and dying world. We are ambassadors for Christ, put here to preach and proclaim the coming kingdom, the good news of the gospel, and the life that is found in Christ and in Christ alone.

In the midst of this sexual revolution, even as we face this gathering storm, Christians must not surrender, either to unbelief or to a hardened heart. Capitulating to this new erotic liberty leads to a capitulation on the essential truths of the gospel itself. We meet revolution with revelation—knowing that God has not left us to figure all this out on our own. We are given God's Word, without which we would have nothing to say on these issues. But God *has* spoken, and so must we. Everything that God reveals is for our good, and for the good of all who will hear and believe. That is our confidence. We have nowhere else to turn.

SEVEN

THE GATHERING GENERATIONAL STORM

The profound shifts and secularization covered thus far spell disaster not only for our present moment but for the generations to come. The secular storm gathers over the youth of Western civilization, and the ominous shadows could not be more troubling. The trends among young people, even within the walls of evangelicalism, will only accelerate the pace of secularization in the years to come. The question remains, how did we get here?

The Rise of Moralistic Therapeutic Deism

Fifteen years ago, Christian Smith and his fellow researchers with the National Study of Youth and Religion at the University of North Carolina Chapel Hill took a close look at the religious beliefs held by American teenagers—they found that the faith held and described by most adolescents came down to something the researchers identified as "Moralistic Therapeutic Deism."

As described by Smith and his team, Moralistic Therapeutic Deism (MTD) consists of beliefs like these: A god exists who created and ordered the world and watches over human life on earth;

that god wants people to be good, nice, and fair to each other, as taught in the Bible and by most world religions. The central goal of life is to be happy and to feel good about one's self, and God does not need to be particularly involved in one's life except when needed to resolve a problem. Finally, good people go to heaven when they die.

That, in sum, is the creed to which much adolescent faith can be reduced. After conducting more than three thousand interviews with American adolescents, the researchers reported that, when it came to the most crucial questions of faith and beliefs, many adolescents responded with a shrug and "whatever."

As a matter of fact, the researchers, whose report is summarized in *Soul Searching: The Religious and Spiritual Eyes of American Teenagers* by Christian Smith with Melinda Lundquist Denton, found that American teenagers are incredibly inarticulate about their religious beliefs, and most are virtually unable to offer any serious theological understanding. As Smith reported,

> To the extent that the teens we interviewed did manage to articulate what they understood and believed religiously, it became clear that most religious teenagers either do not really comprehend what their own religious traditions say they are supposed to believe, or they do understand it and simply do not care to believe it. Either way, it is apparent that most religiously affiliated U.S. teens are not particularly interested in espousing and upholding the beliefs of their faith traditions, or that their communities of faith are failing in attempts to educate their youth, or both.[1]

Their research continued to highlight, "For most teens, nobody has to do anything in life, including anything to do with religion. 'Whatever' is just fine, if that's what a person wants."

The casual "whatever" that marks so much of the American moral and theological landscapes—adolescent and otherwise—is a substitute for serious and responsible thinking. More importantly, it is a verbal cover for an embrace of relativism. Accordingly, "most religious teenager's opinions and views—one can hardly call them worldviews—are vague, limited, and often quite at variance with the actual teachings of their own religion."

The kind of responses found among many teenagers indicates a vast emptiness at the heart of their understanding. Yet teenagers are not inarticulate in general. As the researchers found, "Many teenagers know abundant details about the lives of favorite musicians and television stars or about what it takes to get into a good college, but most are not very clear on who Moses and Jesus were. This suggests that a strong, visible, salient, or intentional faith is not operating in the foreground of most teenager's lives."

One other aspect of this study deserves attention at this point: the researchers, who conducted thousands of hours of interviews with a carefully identified spectrum of teenagers, discovered that for many of these teens, the interview itself was the first time they had ever discussed a theological question with an adult. What does this say about our churches? What does this say about this generation of parents? What does this tell us about the gathering storm of secularism, already drenching the upcoming generations with ambivalent theological beliefs?

In the end, this study indicated that American teenagers are heavily influenced by the ideology of individualism that has so profoundly shaped the larger culture. This bleeds over into a reflexive non-judgmentalism and a reluctance to suggest that anyone might actually be wrong in matters of faith and belief. Yet paradoxically, these teenagers are unable to live with a full-blown relativism, for the researchers note that many responses fall along very moralistic lines—but teenagers reserve their most non-judgmental attitudes for matters of theological conviction and belief. Some go so far as to suggest that there are no "right" answers in matters of doctrine and theological conviction.

The researchers concluded that MTD promotes "a moralistic approach to life. It teaches that central to living a good and happy life is being a good, moral person. That means being nice, kind, pleasant, respectful, responsible, at work on self-improvement, taking care of one's health, and doing one's best to be successful." In a very real sense, that appears to be true of the faith commitment, insofar as this can be described as a faith commitment, held by a large percentage of Americans. These individuals, whatever their age, believe that religion should be centered in being "nice"—a posture that many believe is directly violated by assertions of strong theological conviction.

MTD is also about "providing therapeutic benefits to its adherents." As the researchers explained,

> This is not a religion of repentance from sin, of keeping the Sabbath, of living as a servant of a sovereign divinity, of steadfastly saying one's prayers, of faithfully observing high holy days, of building character through suffering, of basking in God's love and grace, of spending oneself in gratitude and love for the cause of social justice, et cetera. Rather, what appears to be the actual dominant religion among U.S. teenagers is centrally about feeling good, happy, secure, at peace. It is about attaining subjective well-being, being able to resolve problems, and getting along amiably with other people.

Smith and his colleagues recognize that the deity behind Moralistic Therapeutic Deism is very much like the deistic God of the eighteenth-century philosophers. This is not the God who thunders from the mountain, nor a God who will serve as judge. This undemanding deity is more interested in solving our problems and in making us happy: "In short, God is something like a combination Divine Butler and Cosmic Therapist: he is always on call, takes care of any problems that arise, professionally helps his people to feel better about themselves, and does not become too personally involved in the process."

Obviously, Moralistic Therapeutic Deism is not an organized faith. This belief system has no denominational headquarters and no mailing address. Nevertheless, it has millions and millions of devotees across the United States and other advanced cultures, where subtle cultural shifts have produced a context in which belief in such an undemanding deity makes sense. Furthermore, this deity does not challenge the most basic self-centered assumptions of our postmodern age. Particularly when it comes to so-called lifestyle issues, this God is exceedingly tolerant, and this religion is radically undemanding.

As sociologists, Smith and his team suggest that this Moralistic Therapeutic Deism may now constitute something like a dominant civil religion or the underlying belief system for the culture at large. Thus, this basic conception may be analogous to what other researchers have identified as "lived religion" as experienced by the mainstream culture.

Moving to even deeper issues, these researches claim that MTD is "colonizing" Christianity itself, as this new civil religion seduces converts who never have to leave their congregations and Christian identification as they embrace this new faith and all of its undemanding dimensions.

Consider this remarkable assessment:

Other more accomplished scholars in these areas will have to examine and evaluate these possibilities in greater depth. But we can say here that we have come with some confidence to believe that a significant part of Christianity in the United States is actually [only] tenuously Christian in any sense that is seriously connected to the actual historical Christian tradition, but is rather substantially morphed into Christianity's misbegotten step-cousin, Christian Moralistic Therapeutic Deism.

They argue that this distortion of Christianity has taken root not only in the minds of individuals but also "within the structures of at least some Christian organizations and institutions."

This radical transformation of Christian theology and Christian belief replaces the sovereignty of God with the sovereignty of the self. In this therapeutic age, human problems are reduced to pathologies in need of a treatment plan. Sin is simply excluded from the picture, and doctrines as central as the wrath and justice of God are discarded as out of step with the times and unhelpful to the project of self-actualization.

All this means is that teenagers have been listening carefully. They have been observing their parents in the larger culture with diligence and insight. They understand just how little their parents really believe and just how much many of their churches and Christian institutions have accommodated themselves to the dominant culture. They sense the degree to which theological conviction has been sacrificed on the altar of individualism and a relativistic understanding of truth. They have learned from their elders that self-improvement is the one great moral imperative to which all are accountable, and they have observed the fact that the highest aspiration of those who shape this culture is to find happiness, security, and meaning in life.

Secularization and the Impact of Moralistic Therapeutic Deism

This research was presented in 2005. Five years later, in 2010, Christian Smith and another team of associates produced another study called *Souls in Transition: The Religious and Spiritual Lives of Emerging Adults.* The researchers conducted follow-up interviews with 230 of the same individuals included in their first study in 2005. The difference is that these young people were no longer thirteen- to seventeen-year-olds but were instead ages eighteen to twenty-two. Would the age difference also mean a significant shift in religious practice and beliefs?

The answer to that question is both yes and no. In *Soul Searching*, Smith asserted that American teenagers can embody the "highest hopes and most gripping fears" of adults. Indeed, it seems that every generation of teenagers becomes a consuming concern of adults, as well as a target population for sociologists, psychologists, and other researchers. But Smith, in *Souls in Transition*, argued that the more significant research population—and the more determinative age cohort for the future of American religion—may well be the "emerging adults" included in this most recent study.

What to call them? These young people and their life stage have been labeled as "twentysomethings," "youthhood," "adultolescence," and "extended adolescence." Smith chose to use the term offered by psychologist Jeffrey Arnett: "emerging adulthood."

Smith's team asked, "What is it like to be an 18-to 29-year-old in America? What are the major strengths and problems of emerging adults today? How are they faring on their journey to full adulthood?"[2] To these questions they added the religious and spiritual dimensions of the generation. Who are they and what do they believe?

In the first place, they really do represent something new in life stage experience. Their emergence into full adulthood is coming, in the main, considerably later than it did for their parents and virtually every earlier generation after the dawn of modernity. Their emergence into adulthood has been delayed by higher education, by the delay of marriage, by economic instability, and by the continued financial support of their parents. Thus, this generation of young adults has experienced "a historically unparalleled freedom to roam, experiment, learn, move on, and try again."

Following the pattern set by *Soul Searching*, *Souls in Transition* included profiles of several representative young people. They range from the highly conventional and orthodox to the agnostic and atheistic, but most are clustered into a far more ambiguous mediating category.

What has changed since their teenage years? Perhaps the most significant impression presented in the project is that these young adults have distanced themselves from their parents and from their parents' religious faith to a greater degree, though they remain positively related to their parents (and economically dependent upon them) and hopeful about the future of this relationship. They are now preoccupied with life tasks and are struggling to retain optimism amid the baffling array of adult responsibilities before them. They see themselves as broke but are eagerly committed to a consumerist culture.

Above all, they are preoccupied with the concerns of the self. As a matter of fact, Smith, now William R. Kenan Professor of Sociology and Director of the Center for the Study of Religion and Society at the University of Notre Dame, argues that this generation actually has difficulty imagining any objective reality beyond the self. As he explained, "Most have great difficulty grasping the idea that a reality that is objective to their own awareness or construction of it may exist that could have a significant bearing on their lives." To all this he adds that these emerging adults are actually soft ontological antirealists, epistemological skeptics, and perspectivalists, "although few have any conscious idea what those terms mean."[3]

This is a breathtaking observation, yet even Smith seems to underplay what this means for this generation and for the future of American Christianity. These emerging adults are not hardened ideological postmodernists, but their belief systems reveal that a soft form of postmodern antirealism has become part of mainstream culture. Indeed, one of the people quoted in Smith's study, identified as Brad, said, "I mean, I have my beliefs in my head. But I don't enjoy the whole religious scene. I'm not really into it like some people are. I have my beliefs, I believe that's the way it is, and the way it should be, and I go to church every once in a while. But it's kind of low-key."[4]

Brad's comments represent much of Smith's conclusions about the emerging generation of adults. The coming generations do not see themselves as related in any formal or binding sense with churches, formal beliefs, or religious institutions. As Amanda, a young woman highly involved in an evangelical congregation, explains, "Religion is not made for young people."[5]

They are postponing marriage and family formation but definitely not postponing sex. They are playing around, hooking up, and cohabiting. They know that the Bible condemns these behaviors, and they promise themselves that they will one day settle down and adopt a more conservative sexual morality. Like Augustine in his early years, they want chastity, just not yet.

In a haunting and powerful paragraph, Smith explained how this tension between sexual behavior and moral expectation actually distances these young people from their religious and spiritual roots:

> Therefore, emerging adults who are serious about their faith and practice have to do one of three things: choose to reject heavy partying and premarital sex; dramatically compartmentalize their lives so that their partying and sexual activities are firmly partitioned off from their religious activities in a way that borders on denial; or be willing to live with the cognitive dissonance of being committed to two things that are incompatible and mutually denying. Not many emerging adults can or will do any of these things, so most of them resolve the cognitive dissonance by simply distancing from religion.[6]

Accordingly, these young adults are considerably less religious than their parents, less committed to formal doctrines, and less involved, not only in church life, but even in such activities as volunteering in charity work and social organizations.

As for Moralistic Therapeutic Deism, commitment to this belief system remains "alive and well."[7] The main difference between these young people at this stage of life, as compared to their adolescence, is that they now have a larger frame of reference and set of concepts with which to flesh it out.

Writing over twenty years ago about evangelical young adults, sociologist James Davison Hunter of the University of Virginia warned in *Evangelicalism: The Coming Generation* that the generation then in young adulthood—the parents of the generation profiled in *Souls in Transition*—was moving away from the belief that only those who believe in Christ will go to heaven. As he explained, "In the face of intense religious and cultural pluralism in the past century, the pressures to deny Christianity's exclusive claims to truth have been fantastic."[8] Among today's emerging adults, accommodation to that pressure is the rule rather than the exception.

Helpfully, Smith and co-author Patricia Snell point to several factors that encourage emerging adults to remain connected and committed to churches and beliefs—and these have mostly to do with the roles played by parents and other adults in their lives. Young adults who remain closely related to their parents, and who have parents who put a premium on maintaining that relationship, are far more likely to remain both connected and committed. Significantly, their continued commitment also has a great deal to do with the roles played by other adults in a congregation.

Put simply, this is a generation of emerging adults who are struggling to reach full adulthood in the culture of late modernity. They see themselves as needing older adults as allies, mentors, and friends. They know they need help, and they see themselves as facing greater challenges than those faced by their parents. They are not hostile to the faith of their parents, but they are swimming in a very different cultural sea. They are indeed souls in transition, and they seem to know that they are.

The Trend Continues

Smith's sociological work is now almost ten years old—the original participants in his survey are now entering their thirties, which raises a crucial question: Have things changed? Regrettably, the generational storm only intensifies and the trends among Smith's research group and the next wave of young "emerging adults" only reveals far more devastating issues facing Western civilization. Indeed, this generation has become even more self-absorbed, delaying marriage, putting off having children, and rejecting not just Christianity but any religion. What we are witnessing is cultural Christianity in retreat, with radical implications on American public life.

Gerald Seib of the *Wall Street Journal* wrote about the generational trends in a 2019 article titled "Cradles, Pews and the Societal Shifts Coming to Politics: Consequences are big as church attendance declines and the birthrate drops."[9] Seib wrote,

> Sometimes the most important trends—the ones with enormous social and political consequences—are unfolding in plain sight. New data show two of them are under way right now: Americans are going to church less often, and are having fewer babies. Those two trend lines receive relatively little notice, but their social and economic significance is so broad they are worthy of a discussion at this week's Democratic presidential debates and beyond.

Indeed, Seib rightly understands that there are in fact serious implications for a drop in the birth rates and the continued decline of Americans at church. He continued, "The steady, long-term decline in church attendance is confirmed in the most recent *Wall Street Journal*/NBC News poll. Just 29% of Americans now say they attend religious services once a week or more often. That is down from 41% in 2000."

These numbers are staggering and point to a continual generational decay that Smith and his team of researchers originally chronicled in the first decade of the millennium. Seib also stated, "The rise in churchlessness is most dramatic among young Americans. Among those aged 18 to 34, the rate saying they never attend religious services previously was no different from the national rate; now the share of these younger Americans who never attend religious services has more than doubled to 36%." This age range contains the original sample of young adults surveyed by Smith. The consequences of secularization have only intensified. Now, about a third of young adults never set foot inside a church.

Seib argues that these trends will cause seismic social changes in the United States. He wrote, "For generations, churches and synagogues were among the main institutions around which Americans organized their lives. More than just houses of worship, they have been places where Americans unite, find identity and often educate their children. The decline of such communal bonds alters how many Americans identify themselves."

What these numbers reveal is the evaporation of cultural or nominal Christianity. The main evacuation from churches and denominations are casual church members, with thin ecclesiology, little theological conviction, and typically associated with churches in liberal or mainstream Protestantism. Traditionally, people still associated with churches for social, cultural, or even political reasons—those reasons, however, have disappeared. The culture no longer values religious identity.

That said, there is no question that the trajectory of religion in America is on a swift decline. In 2019, Gallup released a major report that included this bottom line: "U.S. church members was 70% or higher from 1937 through 1976, falling modestly to an average of 68% in the 1970s through the 1990s. The past 20 years have seen an acceleration in the drop-off, with a 20-percentage point decline since 1999 and more than half of that change occurring since the start of the last decade."[10]

In my own denomination, the Southern Baptist Convention—a denomination that enjoys the immunity to much of the nation's secularization because of its location in the so-called Bible Belt—has also seen a downward trend in its numbers. Last year, Southern Baptist membership fell to 14.8 million, which is the first time the number dipped below 15 million since 1987. This came as hard news to a denomination that has long prided itself on both size and growth. The numbers, however, don't lie. In 2018, the number of reported baptisms in the SBC stood at 246,442, down from 254,122 in 2017.

Not only does this decline result from diminished evangelistic efforts, it also points to what Seib pointed out in his article in the *Wall Street Journal*, namely, a dramatic drop in childbirths. Seib stated that this problem is equally profound and ominous for American society. Seib wrote,

> The National Center for Health Statistics reported a few weeks ago that the number of babies born in the U.S. last year fell to a 32-year low. Meantime, the general fertility rate—defined as the number of births per 1,000 women aged 15 to 44—fell to the lowest level since the start of federal record keeping. This trend has enormous economic as well as social effects. A declining birthrate means Medicare and Social Security will become even harder to finance over time as fewer new Americans enter the workforce to finance the retirement needs of their elders. The age at which workers can retire may have to be raised, and benefits limited.

Christians today fail to see the reality of childlessness; indeed, we understand that far more is at stake with declining birth rates than merely political or economic upheaval. Historical analyses are very clear: Throughout recent centuries, the vast majority of church members have been the children of church members. It is no accident that falling birth rates are reflected in baptism statistics. There is no question that children raised within Christian homes by Christian parents are most likely to make their own profession of faith and continue in church participation into adulthood. There is also no question that when Christian parents have fewer children, they produce fewer future converts to Christianity. The fall in birth rate has been precipitous and the trend lines parallel baptism statistics in the SBC. In addition to Seib's article, the *Wall Street Journal* editorial board also ran a piece on the declining birth rates among younger generations. The article was titled "America's Millennial Baby Bust," and it reported that the US birth rate has hit a thirty-two-year low.[11] During the period between 1960 and 2017, the US fertility rate (births per woman) was virtually cut in half.

The dramatic fall in the fertility rate began with the development of the oral contraceptive and accelerated with millennials, who delay starting families into their thirties. This is startling news indeed and it all points to a massive generational shift in the American way of life. Seib believes these trends have political consequences and should frame the debate of the 2020 elections. While he is certainly correct, Christians understand the massive theological implications undergirding this generational storm. What does childlessness tell us about the redefinition of human life? What does this tell us about the expectation of the average individual, male or female? What does this tell us about marriage and the glory of the family? What does it tell us about the society? What does it tell us about the future of the church?

The dizzying speed of secularization on the upcoming generation caused much of the rampant childlessness plaguing American society. Secularization altered the understanding of the home and the family as an essential and societal good. The sacredness of marriage, childbearing, and the family is eclipsed by the growing clouds of this secular age. There is a surge in single-child homes as well as homes with no children at all, indicators of an even more rapid permutation of secularization than Smith and his team of researchers could have even imagined in 2005 and 2010.

Where This Storm Could Lead

The coming generations will face never-before-seen challenges in a world that, thanks to the internet and the advent of social media, grows increasingly smaller. Study after study comes out almost daily describing the effects of technology, video games, screen time, and social media on children and young adults. Moreover, the trends witnessed by Smith in his two books early in the millennium have not dissipated but only compounded. Millennials are marrying later, if at all. According to one study, couples between the ages of twenty-five and thirty-four have known each other for an average of six and a half years before marrying—the delay in marriage, however, is not commensurate with a delay in sexual intimacy.[12] Adulthood, once identified as a man and a woman married, raising a family, is now put off well into the third decade of life. Secularization has renegotiated adulthood and marriage, transforming it into an extended phase of adolescence.

Moreover, new research regarding Generation Z points to an even more ominous generational storm than we are witnessing among millennials. Jean Twenge wrote an article in the *Atlantic*, chronicling the downgrade of post-millennials. She queried, "Have smartphones destroyed a generation? More comfortable online than out partying, post-Millennials are safer, physically, than adolescents have ever been. But they're on the brink of a mental-health crisis." Her research revealed that high school seniors in 2015 dated less often than middle schoolers in 2009.

The moral issue at stake is not dating or adolescent socialization. Rather, it is the massive shift away from personal and physical social interaction to a lifestyle completely experienced through a screen.

Courtship has disappeared and the ability to engage in meaningful conversations seems as antiquated as driving a Model T Ford.

Twenge continues,

> Psychologically, [post-Millennials] are more vulnerable than Millennials were: Rates of teen depression and suicide have sky-rocketed since 2011. It's not an exaggeration to describe iGen as being on the brink of the worst mental health crisis in decades. Much of this deterioration can be traced to their phones. . . . The twin rise of the smartphone and social media has caused an earthquake of a magnitude we've not seen in a very long time, if ever. There is compelling evidence that the devices we've placed in young people's hands are having profound effects on their lives—and making them seriously unhappy.

The results of these massive generational shifts cannot be overstated. Indeed, Twenge reveals that cognitive development has declined, with eighteen-year-olds functioning at a fifteen-year-old level and fifteen-year-olds acting more like thirteen-year-olds. In the next decade, humanity will begin to feel the effects of a generation that has not known a world without social media and smartphones—we may not be prepared for the consequences to come.

The issues raised thus far are not the laments of curmudgeons bemoaning this present cultural moment; nor is this chapter a nostalgic exercise, calling for a return to the "good ol' days." The problems facing the coming generations are massive with enormous cultural, social, political, and theological ramifications.

In 2019, David Brooks wrote a column for the *New York Times* with the headline "The Coming G.O.P. Apocalypse."[13] In it, Brooks argued that a generational gap spans the current political land-scape. For Democrats, older voters prefer more moderate candidates while younger voters prefer progressive and socialist candidates.

The bomb in his article, however, comes with this statement: "The generation gap is even more powerful when it comes to Republicans. To put it bluntly, young adults hate them." According to a 2018 Pew survey, which Brooks cites, 59 percent of millennial voters identify as Democrats while only 32 percent identify as Republican. Brooks contends, "The difference is ideological. According to Pew, 57% of millennials call themselves consistently liberal or mostly liberal. Only 12% call themselves consistently conservative or mostly conservative. This is the most important statistic in American politics right now."

These are profound numbers with enormous implications on American public life. These numbers verify a marked and drastic generational shift, namely, the liberalization of America's coming generations. While Brooks considers the political ramifications, Christians understand the theological importance of this generational shift—the increase in liberalization is directly tied to increasing secularization. Delaying marriage, the deconstruction of the family, and the advent of social media have all had both a liberalizing and secularizing effect on America's generations. Moreover, pointing back to Smith's studies in the early 2000s, ascending generations continue to, at an increasing rate, disassociate themselves with any form of religion.

The present generational crisis is the perfect storm of younger Americans rejecting religion, dismantling the foundational institution of Western civilization, namely, the family, and acquiring an addiction to technology and social media. The result of this storm is a secularization and liberalization that multiplies in intensity. The ravages of this storm will only grow as more and more generations continue to depart from any semblance of a traditional family unit. Indeed, the coming generations will completely reject any theistic worldview and religion; not because of an outright hostility toward religion, but because they will probably have never set foot in a church or have any contact with a religious service.

The Gospel and the Next Generation

When faced with unprecedented and overwhelming challenges, fear can paralyze even the most courageous and convictional. The challenges facing the coming generations are perilous, and many of the factors feeding this generational frenzy seem insurmountable. How can Christians and churches reverse the effects of social media? How can Christians show coming generations the glory of family and recapture the spectacular gift of children? How can churches convince sexualized teenagers that God's design for sex is the pathway for true flourishing? How can anyone stop the floods of secularism and liberalism converging in on America's coming generations?

Only the power of the cross and cross-shaped living will stem the tide and dissipate this gathering storm. Christian parents must center their lives on the glory of the gospel and the good news it secures. Lives centered around the cross cast a brilliant light in the midst of a crooked and twisted generation. Faithfulness to God, to his Word, and conviction in the midst of rampant capitulation will provide this generational crisis an alternative path.

Specifically, the church of Jesus Christ must apply the gospel power in at least three ways in order to engage the storm gathering over the coming generations. First, Christian parents must view church as the highest and utmost priority for their family's weekly schedule. We have surrendered Sunday school and youth ministry in many of our churches. I am the product of being involved in the local church many hours a week as a young boy and teenager. My frame of reality was largely set by my parents' design—and it was church whenever the church offered an opportunity, and there were many opportunities: Sunday school, youth choir, Royal Ambassadors (for boys) and Acteens (for girls). There were weekly youth fellowships and youth meetings and regular retreats. There were wonderful and faithful adult volunteers, as well as a faithful youth minister. Christian Smith and his research associates found that one of the distinguishing marks of young people who continue in their church participation as adults was that they had developed a warm and trusting relationship with an adult in the church (even just one) other than their own parents.

How many young people in middle school, high school, or college have that experience today? For many children growing up with Christian parents, the priority of the family is told otherwise. Many Christian parents have bought into the larger culture's portrait of the good childhood, complete with incessant sports activities, violin and ballet lessons, and activities perceived to boost a child's eventual college admissions application. When it comes to church activities with children and teenagers, the scariest words might well be "traveling team." Priorities become clear, both on the part of the church and of parents. Parents can hardly claim shock when their kids grow up and leave what they have never really known. At that point, the opportunity is lost. Exposure to God's people and a gospel-saturated community is essential for the nurturing of children in this secularized age.

Second, Christian parents need to be serious about the effects of technology, screen time, and social media. These commodities can be used for glorious purposes or can destroy. Unrestricted access to technological devices has indeed become an issue of faithful Christian parenting. The ease of access to pornography, specious ideologies, and harmful worldviews can cause enormous harm on a malleable young mind.

Finally, Christian parents must endeavor to fill their homes with the fragrance of the gospel—family worship, family devotions, Scripture memorization, and quality family time will do more to promote the health of the next generation than we can imagine. Inserting spiritually vibrant moments into the family life of a home is essential for the health of impressionable young minds. A myriad of resources is available to equip parents to catechize their children in the truths of God and his Word. How can any Christian parent expect their child to come to know Christ and live a life connected to the people of God if the gospel is never heard or spoken in the home?

In the end, the main point is that every successive generation of young Christians is likely to face even stronger headwinds. The obvious truth is that a church that loses its own young people has no future.

EIGHT

THE GATHERING STORM AND
THE ENGINES OF CULTURE

Culture is the product of a vast array of influences including language and traditions and fundamental worldviews. But cultures are not static, and in the context of hyper-modernism, cultures can change fast—indeed faster than humans have ever experienced.

One of the best-selling books of the 1970s was a book by Alvin and Heidi Toffler entitled *Future Shock*. They argued that our society was experiencing accelerated change at a velocity unprecedented in human history, and that humans were not capable of experiencing so much change, so fast. The "future shock" they described meant "too much change in too short a period of time."[1]

Just keep in mind that *Future Shock* was written before *Roe v. Wade*, before the digital revolution, and before the sexual revolution was transformed into a complete reshaping of the entire society. We are now a culture changing at an alarming speed—and accelerating still.

In one sense, just about everyone contributes something to the direction of the culture, starting in the home and then extending outward to civic involvement and engagement with other people.

We are culture-making cultures. Building a playground is a culture-producing act.

At the same time, given the immense size and scope of our culture, the main drivers of cultural production are the crafters of cultural messaging, and the drivers of the culture are powerful indeed. They produce the entertainment we watch, the media coverage we see, the clothes we wear, the technologies we use, and the education that shapes the minds of young people.

In more recent decades and especially over the last few years, those engines of cultural production have become more openly political and the messaging has been more straightforwardly moral—and in both respects, the main centers of cultural production are pushing hard in a more liberal direction. Our society is not drifting leftward—it is being driven leftward. Our responsibility is to think clearly, carefully, and critically about how our culture is being influenced, and what this means for Christians seeking to live faithfully in a secular age.

The Moral Influence of Hollywood

America thrives on entertainment, and entertainment is one of the biggest businesses on the landscape. Americans are omnivorous consumers of entertainment products. Entertainment drives the culture and possesses enormous sway over American society. It tells the stories that shape the American minds and reach the American heart. Hollywood serves as a cultural factory that mass produces what appears on television and the big screen—and the new screens. But entertainment is never merely entertainment. The cultural products we watch and read and listen to are sending moral messages, constantly. Hollywood controls the narrative, and if you can manipulate the narrative, you govern the mentality, worldview, and character of a culture.

The Oscars represents a clear example of a tool used to promote the narrative influence of Hollywood. The awards show is not only a competition between producers, directors, cinematographers, actors, and actresses but a competition between *narratives*. The Oscars, furthermore, is now overtly political. Hollywood promotes a specific political agenda largely driven by the cultural left, and the Oscars represents the intersection of all the political messaging from Hollywood's elites. As the moral revolutionaries continue to press the culture toward the left, the Oscars becomes more and more a place of cultural negotiation and controversy—no single movie can tick off all the necessary symbolic gestures required by the politics of the moment. The question then becomes, "Which narrative is more compelling? Which narrative pushes the culture further in the moral and political direction desired?"

Hollywood is a cultural industrial complex. It combines the potency of narratives with the power of celebrities to exert a profound and often overwhelming impact on American society. Actors and actresses, like politicians, must outdo one another in political signaling. Each person must strive to stay ahead of the cultural curve—an ever-expanding curve that challenges even the aims of Hollywood and its prominent celebrities.

The power of Hollywood rests in this troubling trend: celebrities have a strong grip on the American conversation. They have the social capital that allows them to influence others—and they are driven by a celebrity culture that now *requires* them to signal their moral precepts and politics, constantly. These celebrities usually have no expertise nor experience in the complex issues to which they speak. Driven largely by the political left, the American cinematic experience has evolved into a highly political event, which attempts to persuade through artistic expression and reveals a very clear moral and political agenda.

Indeed, we have already seen in chapter 3 that Hollywood is ready to twist arms with regards to abortion. When Georgia passed its heartbeat bill, Hollywood responded with a full-broadside, threatening retribution for a state that would dare take a stand to protect unborn life. It is also important to note that the actions taken and threatened against Georgia came not only from actors, actresses, and famous directors; not only from big brand names such as Disney; but also from the guilds representing writers. That tells us that the people who are writing the stories and scripts are just as ideologically committed as the actors—and perhaps more so.

Marxist ideology understood long ago the power of cultural production. By gaining control over the major mechanisms of cultural production, Marxists could coax the masses into adopting its worldview and morality. In the United States, the political left got the message, and even as they were often stymied in bringing about the economic change they desired, they put renewed energy into bringing about massive change through the culture.

The cultural producers and artistic figures have probably tended toward the liberal margins in every culture. In the United States, this was already an issue in the 1930s, and again in the 1950s. Since then, Hollywood and the other manufacturers of culture have embraced that identity and mission. Movie stars and directors, for example, have become agents of the moral revolution—they create a cinematic experience designed for moral persuasion.

All these streams of influence converge at the movie theater. Americans buy their tickets, purchase their popcorn, and take their seats in the theaters generally unaware of the powerful moral message that will soon appear on the big screen. Hollywood utilizes its creative authority to craft compelling narratives in step with the moral revolution—especially the LGBTQ agenda, but increasingly on abortion as well.

Indeed, over the past couple of years, television networks have tripped over themselves as they attempted to cast LGBTQ characters and incorporate the LGBTQ agenda into their shows. Sarah Kate Ellis, the president of GLAAD, set a goal that 10 percent of television characters would be LGBTQ by 2020. Ellis argued, "With anti-LGBTQ policies being debated here and abroad, the stories and characters on television are more critical than ever before to build understanding and acceptance of LGBTQ people."[2] This is a prime example of the moral agenda behind the cultural products consumed by the larger society. The narratives we ingest, the songs we listen to, the images on our screens have a clear, moral agenda.

The storylines powerfully stream across the screen, attempting to move from the eyes of the audience into their hearts. No movie, television show, or song is morally neutral. With artistic sophistication, Hollywood dispenses its agenda around the world—and it's a message we *pay* to watch.

In addition to its moral agenda, Hollywood highlights America's culture of self-congratulation and self-aggrandizement. The Oscars, for example, allots a certain amount of time for the following categories: the program devotes about thirty-seven minutes for film clips about the nominees; thirty minutes for all the speeches; twenty-four minutes for introductions and "banter," and ten minutes for extended applause. Astoundingly, the producers allot about twenty-four minutes for the winners' walk up to the platform—walking up to the platform is a theatrical performance practiced by the winners. All told, the night takes up hours of self-promoting gestures.

Hollywood promotes the moral revolution and basks in its own glory. One of the most interesting aspects of the spectacle is the extent to which the major (and minor) players in Hollywood try their best to signal to one another that they are totally on board with the leading edge of moral and political causes. Their greater fear is that they might seem even a half-step back. There is little hope, realistically, that Hollywood and the vast entertainment complex will slow down their moral messaging. Increasingly, they claim this as their driving program. At the very least, this reminds Christians to be aware of the messages that are being sent, and careful about the narrative we allow into our minds and hearts. Beyond our new cultural consumption, however, we must at least be aware of what the culture at large is watching and the stories that are shaping its direction.

Wall Street and the Moral Revolution

The *Harvard Business Review* enjoys a revered status as a major, mainstream publication that traces the economic shifts that have reshaped American corporate life. Unlike *People* or *Vogue*, the *Harvard Business Review*, or *HBR*, is no faddish magazine. It reports serious developments in the American economy, and it represents a centrist reading of the American corporate culture. Thus, when an article in the *HBR* appears with the headline "Why Many Businesses Are Becoming More Vocal in Support of LGBTQ Rights,"[3] we get the message.

For some time, many American corporations have added their own social capital to the moral revolution, often fueling the agenda of the revolutionaries. Yet, many of these businesses joined forces with the LGBTQ movement *only after* they sensed enough popular support—or, as this article makes clear, enough popular pressure. Indeed, many of the companies joining the moral revolution want to live on the "right side of history," a phrase we hear repeatedly from individuals and institutions who surrender to the demands of the sexual revolution.

Corporate America's desire to build its brand has moved many companies to engage in virtue signaling—a show of support through advertisement or company policies that tilts its hat toward the LGBTQ movement. By sending this signal, companies reveal to the larger culture their place on the "right side of history," and their desire to live as part of the future rather than a now discredited past.

Indeed, Jessica Shortall's article in the *HBR* reveals the vector of the moral revolution in corporate America and how businesses endeavor to extend the parameters of the LGBTQ agenda. Shortall wrote,

> One of the clearer case studies on the intersection of business and social issues is how companies have handled the rise of LGBTQ rights. For many years, businesses have been working to improve their brands and their internal practices on LGBTQ issues investing in culture, benefits, and marketing to welcome LGBTQ workers and customers and to telegraph inclusion and openness. Political activism has been slower and coming. In recent years, however, something has shifted: more companies are speaking up on public policy impacting the LGBTQ community, and many are doing so in places where they face stiff headwinds putting their brands and political relationships on the line—a pointed action in a climate where legal and political debates continue over whether businesses can refuse to serve LGBTQ people.

We are told that the reason for these new directions in corporate America stem from "rapid opinion shifts." The torrent of the sexual revolution has swept up many companies who will protect their brands at all cost—they will do anything to stay on the right side of history. Over the last two decades, corporate America has worked hard to meet the demands of the LGBTQ movement. Companies have established task forces to ensure that they now stay on the right side of the activists of the sexual revolutionaries, who are actively keeping score. Corporations, also influenced by threats of shareholder action, have taken on this kind of activism as part of their stated mission and purpose—an essential part of their corporate branding.

In the *HBR* article, Shortall documented the impact of the sexual revolution on American businesses, citing a 2016 poll, which stated that 50 percent of American meeting planners avoid planning events in states that have passed anti-LGBTQ legislation. She wrote,

"The net approval of same-sex relationships is emerging as a predictor of competitiveness and innovation in cities."

Indeed, recent headlines across the nation have chronicled Amazon's journey to establish its new "HQ2." Cities across the nation fell over themselves in order to demonstrate their friendliness toward LGBTQ policies. Furthermore, companies like Amazon look for "net approval of same-sex relationships." In other words, companies will judge cities and communities on their approval of same-sex relationships. If a city is seen to largely celebrate LGBTQ people, then companies will choose those cities for new ventures, conferences, and meetings because those cities serve as the hubs of innovation and competitiveness. As Shortall argued, "LGBTQ inclusion is good for the economy."

Shortall also reported that many corporations have turned to coalitions with other like-minded companies, which provides support and cover for companies especially in regions of the country where LGBTQ issues are not as popular. This is a "strength in numbers" strategy deployed by corporations who will happily signal virtue for their respective brands and promote ideas that place them on the right side of history—it is a pack mentality that shields companies from a cultural barrage. If a company decided to stand alone against the tides of secularism, they would receive immediate backlash not only from the revolutionaries, but from the coalitions of companies standing with the LGBTQ agenda.

Shortall concluded her article with these words:

> The work of equality requires many voices, and the emergence of the business community as a major force for LGBTQ rights has changed the conversation. Business leaders and the coalitions that convene them will have a game-changing role to play in 2019 and beyond, in the U.S. and around the world. Business competitiveness, the economic strength of their operating environments, and

their commitment to inclusion and diversity demand that they stay the course.

By ending this way, the article shows its true colors: Shortall does not merely offer management advice or offer dispassionate analysis of corporate America—she has moved into advocacy. She sings the song of the moral revolution and summons American businesses to join in the tune. We ought to expect her advocacy for the LGBTQ agenda, given that Shortall led the Texas Competes coalition, which has argued for LGBTQ inclusion in Texas since 2015.

What is shocking is *who* published Shortall's article as well as the *absence* of any controversy or disagreement with the article's claims. This article comes from the *Harvard Business Review*, a mainstream engine in American business culture. The article's appearance in the *HBR* tells us a lot about the direction of this "mainstream" outlet. It tells us a lot about the direction of corporate America.

These developments, revealing as they are, remind us that businesses, especially big businesses, both drive and are driven by the cultural moment. Given the realities of our economy, most businesses are afraid to stray far from the moral comfort zone. Thus, the fact that American business is now a major driver of the sexual revolution, this tells us that the leaders and primary stakeholders in the businesses think that the revolution in morality and sexuality and gender is permanent, unstoppable, and powerful. That point is essential for our understanding.

Two other factors demand our attention. Over and over again we are now told that businesses *must* promote this kind of moral messaging if they want credibility and brand traction with young Americans.

Second, the leaders of the most powerful corporations emerge from the same social environment as the leaders of other cultural sectors—including politics, entertainment, and higher education.

They increasingly share the same worldview aims, and they watch each other carefully.

Silicon Valley and Social Capital

Every major news event has a shadow—and sometimes the real story is hiding in the shadow. It is elusive, it is hidden, but it must be brought to the light in order to fully understand the consequences of any newsworthy development.

A story that demands that kind of closer look came with an announcement by Facebook in May 2019. The social media giant announced that it had banned seven people from using its platform. The *New York Times* reported, "After years of wavering about how to handle the extreme voices populating its platform, Facebook on Thursday evicted seven of its most controversial users, many of whom are conservatives, immediately inflaming the debate about the power and accountability of large technology companies."[4]

Facebook described the evicted users as purveyors of hate whose words had incendiary consequences that potentially could cause violence.

Bret Stephens wrote an opinion piece for the *New York Times* where he said, "The issue isn't whether the people in question deserve censure. They do. Or that the forms of speech in which they traffic have redeeming qualities. They don't."[5]

The individuals booted from Facebook were notorious for dangerous forms of speech, and at least in the eyes of the mainstream media, their "dangerous" messages merited the individuals' forced departure from the world's largest social media platform.

That was the major story; but what is hiding in the shadows of Facebook's announcement?

The *New York Times* report hinted at it in its lead paragraph. Reporters Mike Isaac and Kevin Roose stated that Facebook had for years wrestled with the intersection of free speech and hate speech, concluding that it needed to ban these extreme voices. The key phrase of the *Times* article was the label of these censured voices: "Many of whom are conservatives."

This raises a host of questions, namely, why did Facebook almost exclusively ban conservative voices while leaving many incendiary liberal voices untouched?

The issue gravitates around the word "conservative"—what does the *New York Times* mean when it uses the word in this context?

The definition of a conservative refers to a principle commitment to conservation—to conserving the long-standing institutions and traditions that must be protected and conserved because they are essential to human happiness, health, and flourishing. That represents a classical understanding of "conservative." The *Times*, however, did not employ the word "conservative" in the classical sense. The paper used the word "conservative" but referred to a radical subset of the political right.

The "right" does not equate with conservative. Indeed, the same principle applies to the difference between classical liberalism and the political "left." Yet, the left, usually far left, controls the cultural and creative capital of societies—they possess the platforms, which decide who is allowed in a public forum and who is not. The same is true for ideas. The control officers of modern culture are generally liberal. To them, the left fringe looks far less frightening than the right fringe.

But the reality is actually worse than just described. Liberalism often fails to distinguish between conservatives and the extremists of the right. This can be driven by intention or by carelessness, but the result is the same.

Facebook released a statement that read: "We've always banned individuals or organizations that promote or engage in violence and hate, regardless of ideology. The process for evaluating potential violators is extensive and it is what led us to our decision to remove these accounts today."[6] The *New York Times* reported that

Facebook's move "is one of the tech industry's broadest actions to punish high profile extremists at a time when social media companies are under fire for allowing hateful content and misinformation to spread on their services. It is a politically delicate moment."

This social media age is indeed in a politically delicate moment, and Facebook's decision comes as a massive, precedent-setting move with sweeping moral implications. As the world has moved to platforms like Facebook to stay connected and share information, these freely operated, privately owned companies now have the enormous responsibility of functioning as an arbiter—deciding what speech is allowable speech and what speech is classified as extremist hate speech. Facebook has granted itself a powerful authority to decide which voices will be heard on its platform with a staggering 2.3 billion users.

With a membership amounting to more than a quarter of the world's population, when Facebook bans a user from its website, it effectively removes that individual from a worldwide, cultural conversation.

Facebook, however, finds itself in this moral quagmire. Does it serve civilization to police speech the way Facebook has? This question has perplexed the brilliant minds of human history, especially American history. The founders of the nation enshrined in the First Amendment of the Constitution a guarantee for the freedom of speech and freedom of expression.

Like all the protected rights in the Constitution, there are eventually boundaries, but these boundaries are not easy to define. The Supreme Court can declare that freedom of speech does not permit yelling "fire" in a crowded theater. It is not immediately clear how that principle is to be applied to other contexts and speech. How does a nation that protects the freedom of the press deal with that freedom during a time of war? Is the press free to print information during wartime that would jeopardize a mission or compromise the success of a military campaign?

As perplexing as these questions are, the issue of Facebook only intensifies the confusion. Bret Stephens's opinion column that appeared in the *New York Times* argued that Facebook has no legal obligation to protect free speech by virtue of Facebook's status as a corporation. As a business, it has the right to set its own policies and practices. Facebook functions like a business, not a government bound by a constitution and accountable to the public. On the other hand, one could argue that Facebook possesses more power than many governments on earth, especially with regard to the power of information.

Stephens rightly argued,

> The issue is much simpler: Do you trust Mark Zuckerberg and the other young lords of Silicon Valley to be good stewards of the world's digital speech? I don't, but not because conservatives believe (sometimes with good reason) that the Valley is culturally, politically and possibly algorithmically biased against them. As with liberalism in academia, the left-wing tilt in tech may be smug and self-serving, but it doesn't stop conservatives from getting their messages across. It certainly doesn't keep Republicans from winning elections. The deeper problem is the overwhelming concentration of technical, financial and moral power in the hands of a people who lack the training, experience, wisdom, trustworthiness, humility and incentives to exercise that power responsibly.

Indeed, we do know the predominating worldview that governs Silicon Valley. The overlords of the digital world have made that abundantly clear.

But Silicon Valley finds itself engrossed in a massive political bind. Two competing worldviews arise in this technological, legal, and moral quandary facing social media giants—namely, the European understanding of free speech as opposed to the American model of free speech.

The European tradition of free speech views the right as conditioned by national interests and governmental power. Thus, a right to free speech is more conditional. In some cases, freedom of speech is merely tolerated. An illustration of this would be criminalizing the refusal to use a person's preferred gender pronoun. That's not a hypothetical situation. That is happening in Europe and in Canada.

Those nations, therefore, have exerted pressure on Facebook to clamp down on the types of speech that appear on the platform. Facebook faces a dilemma: either it will comply with European governments and curtail free speech, or the company will face fines, penalties, or even being shut down in those countries.

Meanwhile, the United States presents Facebook with a host of other challenges. Though the nation protects the freedom of speech, will the United States allow Facebook to police themselves, or will the federal government enact legislation to regulate Facebook?

The moral and ethical questions that gravitate around social media are staggering. These social media companies, dominated by a progressive and radically leftist worldview among their leadership, have the power in their hands to shut down any speech they deem hateful and harmful. That means Facebook or Twitter can shut down accounts associated with the pro-life movement. Again, this is not hypothetical. Indeed, during the 2018 midterm elections, Twitter took down a campaign ad for then Congresswoman Marsha Blackburn, when she made reference to actions carried out by Planned Parenthood. The ad was deemed inflammatory and barred from Twitter.

So, this is the story lurking in the shadows. Social media controls the social capital around the world and can bar the use of its service to any person it deems "inflammatory." The seven people evicted from Facebook might be the tip of the iceberg. If Facebook deems *that* speech as hateful, what will stop them from labeling my speech or your speech as hateful? Who draws the lines and who decides what speech should not enjoy protection? Facebook has not even made its criteria clear.

We live in a day when merely opposing abortion or affirming the traditional understanding of marriage as a union between one man and one woman can be labeled as hate speech that causes "harm." Just remember the father in British Columbia charged with "family violence" for refusing to agree with his child's "gender transition." We live in a day where believing that gender is binary is, in itself, identified as harm and violence.

This means that those who hold to a biblical worldview will increasingly find themselves in a precarious position with their use of social media platforms. Those in Silicon Valley have drawn a line in the sand. They are ardently in support of the LGBTQ revolution and promote unfettered access to abortions. Christians may soon find themselves joining the ranks of the evicted for simply holding to a biblically minded worldview and expressing those views on their own social media accounts.

As nineteenth-century historian, politician, and writer Lord Acton famously said, "Absolute power corrupts absolutely."

From a biblical worldview, however, we understand that human sinfulness corrupts power. The centralization and concentration of power—in this case, the power of social media and information—will have disastrous outcomes within free societies.

Facebook has transitioned from a platform allowing for the individual user to connect socially, to a provider of content and information. Facebook produces, edits, and manages its own content. This marks a fundamental shift in Facebook's original intent as a social platform for the user. The rules have changed. Facebook has changed. The entire environment and threats to free speech have changed. Christians bear the responsibility to observe these events and, when necessary, cast a light on the stories hiding in the shadows.

The story from Facebook and other social media giants is not a story of banning violent voices from its platform. No. The story is in the shadows—it is the lurking threat to free speech as we know it, especially speech at odds with the secular agenda.

All this has now erupted in open controversy as Twitter and Facebook have announced policies on "political" advertising. But these policies may be more superficial than first thought. The danger is that viewpoint discrimination will result as all social media giants decide what they will and will not allow—even *who* they will and will not allow to advertise or post. Already, some profile activists have been temporarily blocked or denied access.

The monopolistic power of the social media giants is unprecedented in American history. Add to this the fact that Silicon Valley is rather astonishingly one-sided in its politics, and we can see the huge challenge now facing anyone who holds to a contrary worldview.

"And Then They Are All Mine"

Another major player in the formation of the culture is academia and higher education. An adequate consideration of the role played by the leading American universities and colleges in shaping the culture will take another book, but we must note that the nation's academic culture is now tightly bound to these other culture-driving forces.

The role played uniquely by higher education is revealed when we consider the captive audiences of young people. Increasingly, professors tell us how they see their jobs as agents of cultural change. While many professors see themselves as stewards of the teaching profession and fellow learners with their students, others see their role in very different terms—as agents of ideological indoctrination.

All teaching involves ideology and intellectual commitments. There is no position of authentic objectivity. Every teacher, as well as every student, comes into the classroom with certain intellectual commitments. Some professors set as their aim the indoctrination of students into their own worldview, and many of these worldviews are both noxious and deeply troubling. A professor who acts as such an agent of indoctrination abuses the stewardship of teaching and the professorial calling, but this abuse is more widespread and dangerous than many students and their parents understand.

For Christian parents and students, this should be a matter of deep concern and active awareness. The secularization of most educational institutions is an accomplished fact. Indeed, many college and university campuses are deeply antagonistic to Christian truth claims and the beliefs held by millions of students and their families. Furthermore, the leftist bent of most faculty is well-documented, especially in elite institutions and within the liberal arts faculties. On many campuses, a significant number of faculty members are representatives of what has been called the "adversary culture." They see their role as political and ideological, and they define their teaching role in these terms. Their agenda is nothing less than to separate students from their Christian beliefs and their intellectual and moral commitments.

A good many of these professors deny this agenda, but from time to time the mask is removed. Writing at the "University Diaries" column at the site InsideHigherEd.com, a professor of English revealed this agenda with amazing candor. Responding to an argument about the power of intellectual elites, this professor dropped any effort to hide the real agenda: "We need to encourage everyone to be in college for as many years as they possibly can in the hope that somewhere along the line they might get some exposure to the world outside their town, and to moral ideas not exclusively derived from their parents' religion. If they don't get this in college, they're not going to get it anywhere else."[7]

This professor minces no words. The college experience, the argument goes, is the best (and perhaps last) opportunity for someone to break students' commitments to the moral convictions "derived from their parents' religion."

Similarly, writing in a Seattle newspaper, a teacher of English and college adviser at Northwestern University in Evanston, Illinois, reveals this ideological agenda in even more shocking terms. Bill Savage reacts to the fact that the so-called conservative "red" states are "outbreeding" the "blue" states, which are more liberal in voting patterns. Identifying himself as a political liberal with no children of his own, Savage acknowledges that he and his fellow liberals have a lower fertility rate than conservatives. Nevertheless, he insists that educated urban liberals need not despair. He expresses confidence "that blue America's Urban Archipelago can grow larger, more contiguous, and more politically powerful even without my offspring." How?

"The children of red states will seek a higher education and that education will very often happen in blue states or blue islands in red states. For the foreseeable future, loyal dittoheads will continue to drop off their children at the dorms. After a teary-eyed hug, Mom and Dad will drive their SUV off toward the nearest gas station, leaving their beloved progeny behind."[8]

Then what? He proudly claims: "And then they are all mine."

And then they are all mine. That's right, a significant number of professors are happy to have parents spend eighteen years raising children, only to drop them off on the campus and head back home. These professors are confident that the four or so years of the college experience will be ample time to separate students from the beliefs, convictions, moral commitments, and faith of their parents.

Even after expressing these truly breathtaking agendas, these professors go on to claim that they do not seek to indoctrinate their students into their own beliefs and worldviews, but no one can believe them now.

The college experience is, of necessity, a time for the development of critical thinking. It is a season of tremendous intellectual formation that produces lasting effects. Students should learn the disciplines of critical thinking and analysis, and in this transitional period of life, they will determine whether they will hold to the beliefs and commitments of their parents.

But they should not be subjected to the ideological indoctrination and intellectual condescension that is found in far too many classrooms and on far too many campuses. If nothing else, these remarkable statements of professorial intention should awaken both students and parents to what passes for education within much of higher education. The open hostility and contempt toward Christianity and Christian convictions is truly horrifying.

And then they are all mine. It is hard to imagine words more alarming than those.

NINE

THE GATHERING STORM OVER RELIGIOUS LIBERTY

It was more than one hundred years ago, in the aftermath of the Great War, the war that did not end all wars, that William Butler Yeats sounded the warning in his famous poem "The Second Coming":

> Turning and turning in the widening gyre
> The falcon cannot hear the falconer;
> Things fall apart; the center cannot hold;
> Mere anarchy is loosed upon the world,
> The blood-dimmed tide is loosed, and everywhere
> The ceremony of innocence is drowned;
> The best lack all conviction, while the worst
> Are full of passionate intensity.

That poem was written in 1919 and it voiced for millions a loss of innocence and the evaporation of hope. We can now see that Yeats's words have grown only more prophetic over the last one hundred years. Things are falling apart. The center cannot hold.

We who now live in the late modern age witness a great falling apart, a center that may not hold. The most basic liberties enshrined in our Constitution and cherished throughout all Western civilization are confused, contorted, and sometimes even condemned. The enumerated rights recognized in the First Amendment are now suspect in the eyes of many and injurious in the eyes of others. Religious freedom, freedom of speech, and the freedom of the press, along with the other rights recognized and respected within the Bill of Rights, are all threatened even as other rights are marginalized. Even more distressingly, a new regime of invented rights threatens to replace the rights that are clearly enumerated within the text of the Constitution.

Speaking thirty years ago, Attorney General Meese warned that "there are ideas which have gained influence in some parts of our society, particularly in some important and sophisticated areas that are opposed to religious freedom and freedom in general. In some areas there are some people that have espoused a hostility to religion that must be recognized for what it is, and expressly countered."[1]

Those were prophetic words, prescient in their clarity and foresight. The ideas of which Mr. Meese warned have only gained ground in the last thirty years, and now with astounding velocity. The gathering storm of secularism casts its ominous darkness over essential institutions that promote human dignity, flourishing, and freedom.

The very civilization that paid such an incalculable price through the centuries in order to defend and preserve human rights and human liberty, now grows hostile to the most basic liberty of all. History's most courageous experiment in self-government, predicated upon unalienable rights, now seeks to alienate the unalienable. The cultural left in the United States now dares to use the term "religious liberty" only with scare quotes.

I believe that we have vastly underestimated the reality and comprehensiveness of the challenge we face. We all see parts, but it takes concentrated attention, a devotion to history, and a serious reckoning with ideas to see the whole—the vastness of our crisis. We see religious liberty denied when a cake baker in Colorado experiences sustained efforts to put him out of business (or worse), accompanied nationwide by florists and photographers and a host of others. We see the fire chief of Atlanta, Georgia, removed because he dared to teach a biblical pattern of human sexuality, and then dared to put his convictions into print—primarily for his own church. We see Christian schools and ministries confront unprecedented challenges across several fronts, and we see a continual effort to coerce Christians to surrender to the new regime of sexual rules, gender identity, intersectionality, and identity politics. The enemies of religious liberty are playing hardball, and we were warned.

How could this happen?

We can now see what so many have long denied—that the experiment in liberty and self-government known as the United States of America is premised upon an affirmation of human dignity and human rights that only makes sense within and can only be sustained by a worldview that is based on at least an inherited Christian conception and an affirmation of natural rights.

The Declaration of Independence famously stated this affirmation in the most direct of terms: "We hold these truths to be self-evident, that all men are created equal, that they are endowed by their Creator with certain unalienable Rights, that among these are Life, Liberty and the pursuit of Happiness."

The Founders did not fully understand the affirmation they made, as is clear from the horrible reality of slavery, but they were most certainly correct in their conception of unalienable rights endowed upon every human being by their Creator.

This same spirit gave birth to the First Amendment of the Bill of Rights, without which the Constitution itself would never have been ratified. Religious liberty is the first freedom, the foundational liberty, upon which every other enumerated liberty depends.

But the center is not holding. Religious liberty becomes fragile in a secular age. Indeed, all liberties become fragile in a secular age. The very idea of human dignity will not long survive in a secular season, for once that dignity is grounded in anything other than the act of the divine Creator, human dignity withers to whatever dignity humanity can accord itself. The twentieth century should be warning enough of what happens when human dignity is grounded in a merely secular conception of humanity or dignity.

But religious liberty is also seen as problematic and out of date by those who cherish secular liberty as liberation from the shackles of religious belief, divine revelation, and revealed morality. We live now on the leeward side of a revolution in sexuality and morality that threatens to sacrifice religious liberty as injurious to human freedom, sexual liberty, transgender liberation, and a host of new imperatives. In this view, religious liberty is just another way of allowing religious citizens to threaten the newly declared liberties of those long oppressed and invisible.

Consider the fact that religious liberty is now described as religious privilege. By definition, a privilege is not a right. It can be revoked or redefined as circumstances may dictate. It can be withdrawn or subverted by the courts in the name of liberation and justice. And, in our day, privilege is suspect in the first place—an embarrassment to be identified and corrected.

In 2016 the chairman of the United States Commission on Civil Rights, Martin R. Castro, stated in an official report of the Commission: "The phrases 'religious liberty' and 'religious freedom' will stand for nothing except hypocrisy so long as they remain code words for discrimination, intolerance, racism, sexism, homophobia, Islamophobia, Christian supremacy or any form of intolerance."[2] The commission's report included both religious liberty and religious freedom in scare quotes as if they are merely terms of art—linguistic constructions without any objective reality.

The assault against religious liberty spans every century of human history. This is a fragile liberty that, at any moment, can sink after the sustained barrages of its most ardent opponents. More recently, the assertion of erotic liberty and secularization mark a new chapter in the besiegement of religious freedom—and this chapter presents entirely new, daunting, and deadly challenges to this fundamental human right.

Erotic Liberty v. Religious Liberty

In the oral arguments for the *Obergefell* case, Donald Verrilli, then solicitor general of the United States, was asked if the legalization of same-sex marriage would mean that religious colleges and universities would have to offer same-sex marital housing. Verrilli infamously answered, "It will be an issue." Indeed. It will be an issue. It is an inevitable issue.

We are now witnessing a great and inevitable collision between religious liberty and newly declared and invented sexual liberties. The advocates of same-sex marriage saw this coming, as did the opponents of this legal and moral revolution. Judges and legal scholars also knew the collision was coming. Judge Michael McConnell, formerly a judge of the United States Court of Appeals for the Tenth Circuit and now director of Stanford University's Constitutional Law Center, suggested many years ago that the coming conflict would "feature a seemingly irreconcilable clash between those who believe that homosexual conduct is immoral and those who believe that it is a natural and morally unobjectionable manifestation of human sexuality." Accordingly, he called for a spirit of tolerance and respect, much like what society expects of religious believers and atheists—what he called "civil toleration."[3]

Even though same-sex marriage is new to the American scene, the religious liberty challenges became fully apparent even before it became a reality. Soon after the legalization of same-sex marriage in the state of Massachusetts, several seminars and symposia were held in order to consider the religious liberty dimensions of this legal revolution. The Becket Fund for Religious Liberty sponsored one of the most important of these events, which produced a major volume with essays by prominent legal experts on both sides of this revolution. The consensus of every single participant in the conference was that the normalization of homosexuality and the legalization of same-sex marriage would produce a head-on collision in the courts. As Marc D. Stern, of the American Jewish Congress, stated, "Same-sex marriage would work a sea change in American law." He continued, "That change will reverberate across the legal and religious landscape in ways that are unpredictable today."[4]

Nevertheless, he predicted some of the battlefronts he saw coming and addressed some of the arguments that could already be recognized. Even then, Stern saw almost all the issues we have recounted, and others yet to come. He saw the campuses of religious colleges and the work of religious institutions as inevitable arenas of legal conflict. He pointed to employment as one of the crucial issues of legal conflict and spoke with pessimism about the ability of religious institutions to maintain liberty in this context, for which he advocates. As Stern argued, "The legalization of same-sex marriage would represent the triumph of an egalitarian-based ethic over a faith-based one, and not just legally. The remaining question is whether champions of tolerance are prepared to tolerate proponents of the different ethical vision. I think the answer will be no."[5]

Stern did not wait long to have his assessment verified by legal scholars on the other side of the debate. One of the most important of these, Chai R. Feldblum, presented rare candor and revealed that an advocate for same-sex marriage and the normalization of homosexuality could also see these issues coming. Feldblum pointed to what she described as "the conflict that I believe exists between laws intended to protect the liberty of lesbian, gay, bisexual, and transgender (LGBT) people so that they may live lives of dignity and integrity and the religious beliefs of some individuals whose conduct is regulated by such laws."[6] She went on to state her belief that "those who advocate for LGBT equality have downplayed the impact of such laws on some people's religious beliefs and, equally, I believe those who sought religious exemptions in such civil rights laws have downplayed the impact that such exemptions would have on LGBT people."[7]

This new sexual liberty was invented by moral revolutionaries, was later enshrined by the US Supreme Court, and is now used as a weapon of cultural and legal warfare. Then, looking to the day when same-sex marriage would be legalized, and religious liberty inevitably denied, Feldblum said: "I'm having a hard time coming up with any case in which religious liberty should win. . . . Sexual liberty should win in most cases. There can be a conflict between religious liberty and sexual liberty, but in almost all cases sexual liberty should win because that's the only way that the dignity of gay people can be affirmed in any realistic manner."[8] In other words, there must be no exceptions. Religious liberty simply evaporates as a fundamental right grounded in the US Constitution, and recedes into the background in the wake of what is now a higher social commitment—sexual freedom.

Secularization and Religious Liberty

Secularization rebels against the transcendent, rejects the ontological, and subjectifies every claim to truth. As such, secularization, by its very nature, pits itself against pre-political liberties like religious freedom. For example, in 2018, the California Assembly passed legislation under the guise of consumer protection that would outlaw any transaction that might be related to any claim that sexual orientation or gender identity might be changed. The legislation would explicitly ban the sale of books and other materials that would represent orthodox biblical

Christianity—the consensus of the Christian church wherever and whenever it has been found for two millennia. Assembly Bill 2943, as it is known, is blatantly unconstitutional, but it passed overwhelmingly in the California Assembly, a sign of the times.

Europe, especially in the west and the north, has followed a faster trajectory of secularization as compared to the United States, but the velocity of secular change in our own nation is increasing. The distance between Europe and the United States as measured by secularization is shortening. Keep that ominous reality in mind when you consider that an advocate general for the European Court of Justice advised that religious employers in Europe would see their right to discriminate on grounds of religious belief curtailed. Once again, a legal authority spoke openly of balancing religious liberty and modern individual liberty and he found that religious liberty must give way.

The Economist, hardly a fringe publication, ran the headline: "A Court Ruling Makes It Harder for Faith-Based Employers to Discriminate." The magazine opened the report with these words:

> It is a problem that arises in every liberal democracy that upholds religious belief (and hence, the freedom of religious bodies to manage their own affairs) while also aiming to defend citizens, including job-seekers, from unfair discrimination. As part of their entitlement to run their own show, faith groups often claim some exemption from equality laws when they are recruiting people. To take an extreme case, it would run counter to common sense if a church were judicially obliged to appoint a militant atheist as a priest, even if that candidate was well qualified on paper. But how generous should those exemptions be?[9]

Note the language of the report: "an extreme case," "counter to common sense," "judicially obliged," "militant atheist," "well qualified on paper," "how generous."

We are now down to the question of generosity. How generous will a secular society committed to worship at the altar of sexual liberty be, when deciding whether or to what extent religious liberty is to be respected and recognized?

Just ask the California Assembly, or the European Court of Justice, or the US Commission on Civil Rights, or Commissioner Chai Feldblum of the EEOC.

Or, Americans can ask the proponents of the Equality Act, a momentous piece of legislation, which represents one of the single greatest threats to religious liberty. The Equality Act, now passed by the United States House of Representatives, amends the 1964 Civil Rights Act by including sexual orientation and gender identity as protected classes. In short, the Equality Act explicitly codifies the Christian worldview as hatred, bigotry, and no longer valid as seen by the American legal system. As a consequence, those views have no place in American public life and must only find expression in the most private places of an individual's life—at least for now.

Against the backdrop of the 2020 presidential race, this issue is central and clear. Every major contender for the Democratic nomination supports the Equality Act; and, the Democratic Party also aims to retake the United States Senate. If they maintain the House, regain the Senate, and secure the presidency, Democrats will have all they need to unleash a full-scale assault against religious liberty by making the Equality Act law. Indeed, the extent of Democratic support for the Equality Act was on full display during a CNN LGBTQ Presidential Town Hall in October 2019, which featured the main contenders for the Democratic nomination for president of the United States. What America witnessed that night was a moral, political, and cultural earthquake. The rhetoric of the candidates finally stated clearly the intention of a Democratic Party sold out to the most radical proposals of the sexual revolution.

A particular exchange between CNN anchor Don Lemon and former Congressman Beto O'Rourke revealed the extent to which contenders for the Democratic nomination will go to deconstruct religious liberty in the name of the newly declared sexual liberties. Though O'Rourke's candidacy failed, his answers that night represent the trajectory of the Democratic Party's view of religious liberty.[10]

Lemon asked O'Rourke, "This is from your LGBTQ plan, this is what you wrote: 'Freedom of religion is a fundamental right, but it should not be used to discriminate.'" Lemon then pressed the question: "Do you think religious institutions like colleges, churches, charities, should they lose their tax-exempt status if they oppose same-sex marriage?" Without skipping a beat or drawing a breath, O'Rourke answered, "Yes." After that "Yes" came momentous applause from the studio audience. O'Rourke went on to say, "There can be no reward, no benefit, no tax break for anyone or any institution, any organization in America that denies the full human rights and the full civil rights of every single one of us. So as president, we're going to make that a priority and we're going to stop those who are infringing upon the human rights of our fellow Americans."

O'Rourke's answer dropped like a neutron bomb on the American political landscape and is indeed the clearest picture yet of the collision between religious liberty and sexual liberty. The dismantling of religious liberty for the sake of LGBTQ liberty has long been the trajectory of the secular age—but after the Town Hall, it is clear that the Democratic Party is fully on board.

As discussed above, Donald Verrilli, during the *Obergefell* oral arguments, quipped that claims of religious liberty "will be an issue" for Christian colleges or universities who refuse to alter their sexual ethics and religious convictions. That "*will*" was a future tense. After the CNN Town Hall, however, we are now speaking in the *present* tense. O'Rourke positioned himself, to the sound of thunderous applause, as an open threat to religious liberty. He publicly declared that he will strip religious organizations, even *churches*, of their tax-exempt status if they refuse to adopt his secular orthodoxy.

While O'Rourke was the only candidate who used such explicit language, the other candidates offered similar positions, veiled behind more politically acceptable rhetoric. Still, the trajectory of the Democratic Party is such that no potential nominee for president could ever walk back a statement like this, not even a millimeter.

Indeed, shortly after the Town Hall, O'Rourke tweeted his statement, as if proud of his rhetoric. He made it clear that he did not intend to walk back his statement until twenty-four hours later, when he said that he did not want to remove tax-exempt status for religious institutions and churches merely for their *beliefs*—he would, however, deny tax-exemption for *discriminatory* actions. The press seemed satisfied with this "clarification." O'Rourke's explanation, however, in no way abrogates his brazen rhetoric during the CNN Town Hall. Indeed, the intersection of beliefs and practices is exactly where the battle is being waged for religious freedom. Can Christian institutions, schools, or congregations for that matter, *act* in accordance with and not contrary to its own theological *beliefs*?

The battle for religious liberty does not exist in some hypothetical, dystopic future. The collision between religious freedom and the newly declared erotic liberties clashed on prime-time television. Each and every candidate during CNN's Equality Town Hall, in one way or another, unleashed a full broadside against the most essential quality and virtue of any government or civilization, namely, the freedom of the conscience.

During the Town Hall, each candidate for the Democratic nomination was allowed thirty minutes, and the night's charade began with New Jersey senator Cory Booker. Booker was asked, "How would you address the, at times, juxtaposing issues of religious freedom and LGBTQ rights?" Booker responded, "It's a great question, and thank you very much. Look, this is something I've been dealing with all my life. . . . And so, for me, I cannot allow as a leader that people are going to use religion as a justification for discrimination.

I can respect your religious freedoms but also protect people from discrimination."

This is the same stance articulated later in the night by Beto O'Rourke, only slightly more veiled behind the idea of "discrimination." In essence, the New Jersey senator will champion religious freedom *until* it actually means anything.

Immediately thereafter, Senator Booker called for the passage of the Equality Act, which the House of Representatives passed earlier this year. The Act accomplishes exactly what Booker and O'Rourke articulated during the Town Hall—it ends all discrimination on the basis of LGBTQ identity without any adequate provision for religious liberty. Thus, because each candidate during the Town Hall supports passage of the Equality Act, they effectively support the same argument made by O'Rourke, just without the candor and honesty.

CNN's Dana Bash asked Senator Booker, "Do you think that religious education institutions should lose their tax-exempt status if they oppose LGBTQ rights?" The senator responded, "We must stand up as a nation to say that religion cannot be an excuse to deny people health insurance, education and more." Again, what must be noted is that "education and more," affirms the stripping of tax-exempt status to any Christian institution that maintains biblical principles and holds fast to its theological conviction.

Then, Booker was pressed with the follow-up question: "So, would they lose their tax-exempt status?" The senator responded, "Again, I, I will press this issue, and I'm not, I'm not saying, because I know this is a long legal battle, and I'm not dodging your question, I'm saying that fundamentally that discrimination is discrimination." If he didn't dodge the question, he certainly squirmed, not wanting to say out loud the essence of his position, namely, the reduction of religious liberty and all the freedoms protected in this constitutional right. Indeed, for Senator Booker, if religious conviction conflicts with his political stance, then it is deemed discriminatory.

After Senator Booker, former vice president Joe Biden took the stage, where he declared, "I suspect . . . this is going to be one forum where you're going to get very little disagreement among the Democratic candidates. I'm proud of the position they all have because every one of us, if there are differences, they are just in degree and emotional concern."

It is difficult to know exactly what the vice president meant by those words—at the very least, it appears to be a way to catch himself up with the dizzying pace of the left wing of his party, which threatens to leave him behind. Indeed, during his thirty-minute segment, the vice president told a lengthy story of his childhood, aiming to show that he has never harbored discriminatory feelings toward homosexuals because, since his boyhood, he's supported LGBTQ issues. In other words, he tried to position himself as way ahead of the curve on same-sex marriage and the LGBTQ movement—that he did not have to evolve on these issues like other Democrats. But this is not honest, of course. Mr. Biden did not support same-sex marriage until it was politically expedient to do so, and that was true for figures like former presidents Bill Clinton and Barack Obama, as well as former secretary of state and the 2016 Democratic nominee for president of the United States, Hillary Clinton. All of them "evolved."

After the vice president came Pete Buttigieg, the mayor of South Bend, Indiana, and the only openly gay candidate running for president. Indeed, he is the only candidate married to an individual of the same sex.

Hours before the Town Hall, Buttigieg released an entire platform on LGBTQ issues entitled "Becoming Whole: A New Era for LGBTQ+ Americans." At eighteen pages long, it includes a laundry list of every goal of the LGBTQ movement, as well as some interesting items like, "Expand the representation of LGBTQ people and history in our national park system." No one can accuse Mayor Buttigieg of leaving anything out.

During the Town Hall, CNN anchor Anderson Cooper asked him about religious liberty. Buttigieg stated, "Religious liberty is an important principle in this country, and we honor that. It's also the case that any freedom that we honor in this country has limits when it comes to harming other people. We say that the right to free speech does not include the right to yell fire in a crowded theater. And the right to religious freedom ends where religion is being used as an excuse to harm other people."

Harm means any kind of policy or action that could be perceived as discrimination against LGBTQ people. This would include a Christian college requiring its faculty to hold to certain doctrinal convictions as well as requiring faculty and students to live by a certain biblical, moral code.

Moreover, Buttigieg tried to present himself as the new icon of the theological left in the United States. Indeed, theological issues arose during Buttigieg's time when Anderson Cooper asked him, "Is being gay a sin?" The mayor responded, "I don't believe it is. I also get that people reach their own understandings of their own faith. I guess where I try to reach people is that, can we at least agree that whatever faith tradition or commitment they have agrees with mine? That we are called to compassion? That we are called to seek out in one another what is best? And that we are supposed to protect those who are vulnerable?"

Mayor Buttigieg, in a few words, concocted his own theology—he just made up his own religion. While he claims a Christian identity, *nothing* he attests remotely resembles orthodox, biblical Christianity. Homosexuality is declared to be not a sin because Pete Buttigieg does not want it to be a sin. He simply ignores the Bible.

After Mayor Buttigieg came Senator Elizabeth Warren of Massachusetts. During her time, a member of the audience asked her what she would do if a supporter approached her and said, "Senator, I'm old-fashioned, and my faith teaches me that marriage is between one man and one woman. What is your response?"

Senator Warren shot back with a condescending putdown that was widely celebrated in the press and clearly loved by the audience at the Town Hall. She said, "Well, I'm going to assume it's a guy who said that, and I'm going to say, 'Then just marry one woman. I'm cool with that.'" Then, during the loud applause that broke out, she quipped, "Assuming you can find one." Laughter erupted in the auditorium.

At the time of the Town Hall, Senator Warren enjoyed front-runner status. The front-runner for the Democratic nomination for president of the United States condescendingly said to Americans, in effect, "If you do not hold to my view of marriage and homosexuality, you are not even worthy of anyone marrying you." It should tell us a great deal that this kind of sentiment is applause worthy for millions of Americans. In short, if you will not capitulate to the sexual revolution, then you are so backward that you do not even deserve to be married yourself. No one should want to marry you.

Following Senator Warren was Senator Kamala Harris of California. She was questioned by CNN anchor Chris Cuomo and in the first few seconds of her interview, Cuomo found himself in an explosive situation that went viral on social media.

Senator Harris walked onto the stage after being introduced and said, "My pronouns are *she, her,* and *hers.*" This is a nod to the semantics of the LGBTQ movement, which views gender pronouns not as contingent upon one's biological sex, but however one subjectively identifies. It is a way to "honor" the dignity of an individual who wants to be identified as either male, female, or any other fanciful identity on the chaotic spectrum of the LGBTQ sexual ethic.

Cuomo, attempting to make a joke, simply said, "Mine too," with a quizzical look on his face. Harris responded, "All right." The days following the Town Hall, Cuomo attempted to overcome this enormous gaffe that just may cost him the liberal influence and stature he worked so hard to build over his media career.

He should have known the trouble he put on his own shoulders when he made a joke with pronouns, especially with the militancy of the LGBTQ movement. Indeed, reports around the globe detail the consequences of those who will not capitulate to the new sexual ethics demanded by transgender activists. In the United Kingdom, a doctor lost his job over failure to recognize an individual's self-prescribed pronouns. In the United States, a teacher lost his job because he would not refer to a transgender student by that student's preferred gender pronoun. Chris Cuomo, attempting to recover his image, may receive a pass from the LGBTQ activists, but only because he's practicing the art of groveling.

While Cuomo's gaffe stole the attention away from his segment with Kamala Harris, it is important to note that the California senator, like all the candidates that night, declared her unwavering support of the Equality Act—a piece of legislation she said would be her top priority to pass. Again, the legislation, in its current form, has *no* provisions or considerations for religious liberty.

After Senator Harris came Beto O'Rourke. His session, given its importance, will be covered in detail below. After the former congressman, Democratic senator Amy Klobuchar of Minnesota—identified as something of a moderate—positioned herself exactly in line with even the most radical elements of the LGBTQ movement.

Her first priority is the passage of the Equality Act, which will deny the rights of conscience to Christians, religious businesspeople, and even religious institutions and schools that will not recognize the new secular orthodoxy. She attempted to veil this destruction of religious liberty with a friendly demeanor and beaming smiles. Indeed, she made her stance clear when she said, "First of all, our Constitution, as you know, has been founded on a separation of church and state, and we can have different faiths in this country, but the law rules. And the law rules when it comes to discrimination and all kinds of other things. I can just tell you that I will appoint Supreme Court justices that understand that. That's number one." Case closed.

Moreover, during Senator Klobuchar's segment, an important issue came up for many Democrats: the distinction between *good* religion and *bad* religion. Good religion is liberal religion, a set of beliefs in lockstep with the LGBTQ revolution. Klobuchar identified with it personally, declaring that she identified with a United Church of Christ congregation and, "That is the faith that I raise my daughter in and what I grew up in the last few years."

Don Lemon then asked, "So, on that subject, should the federal government give funding to any religious non-profit organizations that oppose same-sex marriage? For example, an adoption agency that won't work with LGBTQ parents?" She immediately said, "Yeah. I think that you've got to have agencies that follow the law, and that's one of the reasons that I want to pass the Equality Act, I think that's really important." Even Senator Klobuchar, often identified as a moderate, holds essentially to the same position clearly articulated by Beto O'Rourke.

Former cabinet member Julián Castro also promoted the good religion versus bad religion dichotomy, even though he identifies as a Roman Catholic. Castro indicated that there are plenty of Roman Catholics who agree with the LGBTQ revolution, though he failed to mention that such positions fly in the face of the official doctrines of the Roman Catholic Church. Once again, only *good* religion can be affirmed. Official Roman Catholic dogma is anathema because it remains outside the orthodoxy of the LGBTQ revolution.

The final figure on the stage was Tom Steyer, a billionaire candidate who was making his first major appearance as a Democratic candidate at the Town Hall. Steyer identified a mass generational shift happening in the American public. He said to LGBTQ activists, "Don't worry. Everything is going your way. It's a matter of generational inevitability." This "generational inevitability" led Steyer to advocate for term limits on members of the United States Congress. He said, "If they are replaced by younger people, they are almost assuredly going to be in agreement with you."

Nothing, however, competed with the candor of Beto O'Rourke. Must churches and institutions that will not adhere to the newly prescribed sexual orthodoxy lose their tax-exempt status? He was ready with the simple answer "Yes." No equivocation. No "politically correct" veil of obscure rhetoric.

The first chief justice of the United States Supreme Court said that the power to tax is the power to destroy. That's what is at stake in O'Rourke's answer.

On the left, O'Rourke met some opposition—not because they disagreed with his position, but because he let the cat out of the bag.

Michael McGough, senior editorial writer for the *Los Angeles Times*, ran an article with the headline "Beto O'Rourke's 'Church Tax' Idea Plays into Conservative Paranoia About Same-Sex Marriage."[11] Interestingly, McGough described conservative evangelicals as paranoid—probably because we actually listen to the words spoken by those who aspire to the highest office in the United States and the leaders of the Democratic Party. What McGough calls *paranoia* might otherwise be called *reality*.

The *Los Angeles Times* article states, "So it would seem from O'Rourke's answer on CNN that if he had his way, the Catholic Church would lose its tax-exempt status unless it changed its teachings about marriage." Then, McGough stated, "The idea that the legalization of same-sex marriage would lead to curtailment of religious freedom has long been floated by conservatives."

This is categorically false. The shackling of religious freedom is not merely a fear of the religious right but a point of advocacy by the cultural left. It was the Obama-appointed solicitor general of the United States who stated, before the Supreme Court, that claims of religious liberty would be an issue in a post-*Obergefell* United States. Mark Tushnet, a Harvard Law professor, unabashedly declared, "The culture wars are over. They lost, we won."[12]

Tushnet continued, "For liberals, the question now is how to deal with the losers in the culture wars. That's mostly a question of tactics. My own judgment is that taking the hard line, you lost, live with it, is better than trying to accommodate the losers who, remember, defended and are defending positions the liberals regard as having no normative pull at all. And taking a hard line seemed to work reasonably well in Germany and Japan after 1945."

The William Nelson Cromwell Professor of Law at the Harvard Law School said that conservative Christians, traditional Roman Catholics, Orthodox Jews, and Muslims who cannot join the sexual revolution ought to receive the treatment of a defeated foe, akin to the treatment of Germany and Japan after World War II. This is not misguided paranoia from religious conservatives. These are *the* words of the left.

In the aftermath of the Town Hall, a spokesperson for the O'Rourke campaign said, "Of course Beto was referring to religious institutions who take discriminatory action. The extreme right is distorting this for their own agenda."

This statement appeared in an article by the editorial board of the *Dallas Morning News*. The article went on to report,

> O'Rourke's stance invited accusations from the right that in his drive for tolerance, he would punish religious groups that disagree with him, and is therefore pushing intolerance. The outpouring from gay rights activists was enthusiastic, though some commentators warned that O'Rourke is only feeding into the suspicion some conservative Christians hold toward Democrats and their sense of persecution.[13]

It is at this point that I want to offer an important challenge to the other candidates vying for the Democratic nomination: If this is not your position, I dare you to say so. I dare any of these candidates to state that O'Rourke was wrong—that religious belief cannot be disjoined from religious action; that the government cannot, by virtue of its own Constitution, infringe upon the freedom of the conscience and religious conviction.

I imagine that not one of the leading candidates will walk back O'Rourke's position to the slightest degree. They may use different language or say that O'Rourke may not have understood the implications of his language. They will evade the question and soften their tone, but make no mistake, they will hold fast to the mores of the LGBTQ revolution—they have no choice in a Democratic Party that is sprinting toward the left.

Our constitutional order roots every successive right in the priority of religious liberty. The religious liberty clauses of the Constitution are more basic than any other among the enumerated rights. But, we would expect, when the most basic of all rights is threatened, so eventually are all others.

Furthermore, we find a basic moral and realistic logic of liberty within the First Amendment. We also find an interdependence of liberties. Thus, we should not be surprised that the freedom of speech and freedom of the press are also at risk. Americans are often shocked and even offended by the claims that free speech is often denied, but on many of our most elite college and university campuses, free speech is dismissed as a bourgeois value. The University of California at Berkeley—the very campus where the Free Speech Movement was born in the 1960s—has now grown hostile to free speech, with many students and faculty arguing that freedom of speech renders the campus "unsafe."

And for far too many, freedom of the press means freedom for the press they like, an impulse that can appear on both the right and the left. But freedom of the press means the freedom to print, publish, broadcast, post, and communicate as a logical and necessary extension of freedom of speech. Without freedom of the press, the populace is force fed and misled, increasingly unable even to recognize the truth, and freedom of speech disappears.

It will be an issue for every Christian school, college, or university. It will be an issue for every Christian in the professions, in business, in public service, in uniform. It will be an issue for us all, and particularly for our children and their children and their children's children.

The agents of coercive secularism evidently believe that the American public will not be safe until the last religious symbol is pried off of the last square inch of public property. Secularization lost some notable battles over the Peace Cross in Bladensburg and the cake baker Jack Phillips. Its loss, however, in no way limits its continued zeal to see religious liberty cut down to size in American public life.

In response, I posit that we cannot understand the transcendent value of religious liberty without these three essential words: God, truth, and liberty, and in that order. Every one of these words is indispensable. Each of these words is controversial. There can be no lasting defense of religious liberty without understanding how these three words hold together. Only by recapturing the meaning of these words and inserting them into this secular moment can Christians manifest a powerful apology for religious liberty—a liberty necessary for the flourishing and continued security of Western civilization.

God

Aleksandr Solzhenitsyn once spoke of hearing older Russians explain the disasters their nation had experienced in the twentieth century. They stated, "Men have forgotten God; that's why all this has happened." I remember older Americans citing these words of Solzhenitsyn, one of the bravest voices of any age, as they explained Soviet tyranny. But these words ring differently in my ears now. We are living in our own age of threatened liberties. Men have indeed forgotten God, and that is why all this has happened.

We are living in an age of accelerating secularization. The causes and courses of secular motion are debatable, but the essential truth is beyond question. Belief in God, any theistic belief, is in eclipse.

This is especially true among the intellectual elites and the cultural creatives. Decades ago, Yale law professor Stephen Carter argued that the intellectual elites had reduced God to a symbol and religion to a hobby. Now, those same elites see God as a dangerous symbol and religion as a scandalous hobby.

Consider the argument made by Frank Bruni, columnist for the *New York Times*. He just put into concise words what many in the political class have been saying for years—that religious liberty is to be tolerated so long as believers keep their religion in their hearts, homes, and pews. No public significance. Keep your religious beliefs where they belong, out of public view. That is the denial of religious liberty.[14]

I am not arguing that there can be no defense of religious freedom among unbelievers. I am not arguing that there were no Deists among the Founders. I am arguing that there can be no sustained defense of religious liberty without intellectual respect for belief in God and cultural respect for religious devotion. Even when Americans claim to rest their argument for liberty, for human rights and human dignity on a secular foundation, they are actually borrowing intellectual capital from Christianity. Even their form of non-theism requires the inheritance borrowed from theism. But I fear—and fear is the right word—that we are witnessing the collapse and retreat of any secular notion of human rights and human dignity that would include religious liberty.

Truth

I believe that this word might actually be the most neglected of the essential vocabulary of the Declaration of Independence. "We hold these truths to be self-evident," they stated, "that all men are created equal, that they are endowed by their Creator with certain unalienable Rights, that among these are Life, Liberty and the Pursuit of Happiness."

Every one of these words demands our rapt attention, but do not move too quickly over the word "truths." A defense of religious liberty (and all other self-evident liberties) is predicated upon an assertion of truth—not mere opinion, or judgment, much less "values." The worldview that will alone sustain liberty is a worldview that is established upon a defense of truth—the objective existence of reality and the necessary correspondence of statement and objective truth.

Why would we expect an academic and elite culture now pervasively shaped by postmodern notions of truth to defend religious liberty? If objective reality does not exist or cannot be known, then politics is reduced to what Harvard professor Mary Ann Glendon correctly calls "rights talk." Politics collapses into nothing more than an endless succession of battles over contested "rights."

The modern denial of truth as real and knowable reminds us of the prophetic warning of theologian Francis Schaeffer, who argued a half century ago that those who believe in objective truth would have to declare our belief in "true truth." The American Patriots declared their belief in truth, not only in objective reality, but in the self-evident truths for which they were willing to sacrifice their lives, their property, and their personal honor. These truths were their bold argument, not these opinions, these values, or these social constructs. No truth, no liberty.

The postmodern, social-constructivist, non-realist view of truth is hardly debated in mass culture any longer—not because it is so rare but because it is everywhere. Driven by academia and those who create the cultural capital, it has become the atmosphere of American life. But if there is no true truth, there are certainly no self-evident truths, and the foundation of the American experiment in liberty—including religious liberty—disappears.

Liberty

The Founders not only asserted truth claims—they defended liberties. They went further to argue that the proper function of government is "to secure these rights." To secure them, not to invent them, or to create them, or even to discover them. Instead, the function of government is to secure rights and liberties that pre-exist the government, and certainly pre-exist the state. Religious freedom is truly the First Freedom, for without this prior freedom all others become fragile and contingent.

As a Christian theologian, I would ground that First Liberty in the very first chapter of the very first book of the Bible. The book of Genesis tells us that God created human beings in his own image, each a living soul. Human dignity is grounded in the loving and glorious creation of the self-existent, omnipotent, all-glorious God, who revealed himself perfectly—incarnationally in Jesus Christ, verbally in the holy Scriptures, and clearly even in the very structures of creation. We owe every human being, created in God's image, the full recognition of human dignity and the sacredness of every human life—including life in the womb.

Make no mistake. These issues are not unrelated. The right to life and the right to exercise liberty, including religious freedom, are deeply related. It is no accident that a society that devalues life in the womb will also devalue religious liberty. If we are cosmic accidents and there is no inherent meaning to our lives, then there is no sacredness to human life—any human life—and liberty is just another word for my preference over yours. The eclipse of the biblical worldview makes every arena of life deadly and dangerous—from the womb to the classroom to the courtroom to the bedroom.

Conclusion

God, truth, and liberty. We need to discipline ourselves to say these words together. We must teach them to our children and to our neighbors. We must cherish them in our schools and in our homes; and teach them in our churches. The great challenge to religious liberty in our times is no threat at all to liberal religion. Those churches and denominations have long ago surrendered to the moral revolutionaries, and they simply do not believe anything sufficiently theological to get any of them into trouble. They can afford to put quotation marks around religious liberty.

We must defend the right to believe in enough theology to get us into trouble with anyone, anywhere, in a secular age. We must defend the right of Christians, along with all other believers, to be faithful in the public square as well as in the privacy of our own homes, hearts, and churches. We must defend the right to teach our children in the nurture and admonition of the Lord. We must defend the rights of Christian schools to be Christian—and to order our institutions around the Word of God without fearing the crushing power of the state. We must defend the right of generations of those yet unborn, to know the liberties we have known and now defend.

Oddly enough, this will mean defending florists and cake bakers and fire chiefs, and pharmacists, and teachers, and preachers, and moms and dads who dare to resist the secular powers that be.

These are days that will require courage, conviction, and clarity of vision. We are in a fight for the most basic liberties God has given humanity, every single one of us, made in his image. Religious liberty is being redefined as mere freedom of worship, but it will not long survive if it is reduced to a private sphere with no public voice. The very freedom to preach the gospel of Jesus Christ is at stake, and thus so is the liberty of every American. Human rights and human dignity are temporary abstractions if they are severed from their reality as gifts of the Creator. The eclipse of Christian truth will lead inevitably to a tragic loss of human dignity. If we lose religious liberty, all other liberties will be lost, one by one. No God, no truth. No truths, no liberty. No liberty, and nothing remains but the heel of someone's boot.

Those who signed the Declaration of Independence pledged

to each other their lives, their fortunes, and their sacred honor. Indeed, the Declaration of Independence, our most foundational national charter, spoke of "the Laws of Nature and of Nature's God." We should not over-read this statement, but we dare not under-read it. The Founders claimed an authority higher than themselves and natural rights and liberties that were pre-political, pre-constitutional, pre-governmental, and prior to our own respect. When belief in God recedes, the only secure ground of human rights and human dignity recedes as well. Solzhenitsyn had it right. You ask how this happened. Men have forgotten God. That is how all this has happened.

The Declaration of Independence expressed the convictions of this nation in stating boldly that we hold these truths to be self-evident. *We hold these truths.* These truths, not mere opinions or beliefs. Held, not merely asserted or argued. To hold is to exercise a stewardship. We hold these truths, not merely for ourselves and for our time, but for our children, and our children's children, and all those who will become a part of this grand experiment in self-government. But we also hold these truths for the world and before the world. Such a stewardship requires the defense of these truths, the careful definition of these truths; truths that should be, but often are not, recognized as self-evident.

The First Amendment will not save us. Without prior and enduring commitment, the text is only words on paper. As Christians, we give thanks to God alone, who made us in his image, gives us life, and endowed us with these rights. Only Jesus Christ can save, and he saves to the uttermost. That is the great good news. The sacred freedoms we cherish secure our right to worship God in spirit and in truth, to tell the good news of the gospel of Jesus Christ, and to teach the whole counsel of God.

The First Amendment will not save us, but it now falls to us to save the First Amendment.

CONCLUSION

Into the Storm

Winston Churchill's prophetic warnings were ignored in the 1930s, where he walked alone through what have been called his "wilderness years." By the end of the same decade, Churchill would be proved right and Europe had plunged madly into another horrifying war—the war more horrifying and deadly than all previous wars in human history. The great tragedy of the 1930s was that so many failed to take the threats seriously. The democratic nations of Europe had allowed themselves to become deluded, yet again. When the reality dawned on them, it was too late.

My reference to Winston Churchill is not meant to evoke military metaphor and extend it beyond reason. We are now in a battle of ideas, and we will be in this battle until Jesus comes. But the example of Churchill has haunted me since I was very young and first came to consider his place in history and his prophetic role. I do not want to miss the storm that is gathering, and there can be no doubt that we are facing a gathering storm. By now it is clear that this storm is real and that it cannot be avoided. The one true God is Lord over history, and he has now called Christians in this generation into the storm.

Every chapter of this book sought to reveal the gathering storm of the secular age and its consequences for every sphere of society. The dechristianization of the culture—the severing of modernity from a biblical worldview—has dehumanized babies in the womb, redefined marriage, fractured the family unit, and promoted a radical sexual revolution, which fundamentally alters not only the way human beings live but even our understanding of what it means to be human. For Americans, the intensity of this storm picks up with the backdrop of a presidential election. An election serves as a pressure chamber, forcing all important issues to the surface. All the issues from marriage, human life, abortion, family, education, and sexuality come to the fore in an election cycle.

Christians must realize that the more enduring contest is not between rival candidates but between rival worldviews. A clash of worldviews reveals all the fault lines of a society, from education and economics, to arts and entertainment. Eventually, everything is at stake. Over time, every culture conforms in general terms to one worldview, not to more than one. One morality, one fundamental picture of the world, one vision of humanity prevails. One central challenge for Christians is to maintain hope and joy and full faith when the culture appears to be hardening against us.

Of course, denial is not a strategy. The sad fact is that we have seen our society abandon moral sanity on issue after issue. We also learn that part of this is our own responsibility. Even if we failed in the past, we cannot afford to fail now.

I believe that Christians bear the highest responsibility in this secular age. Just consider what is entrusted to us. We know the true foundation of human dignity and human rights. We know *why* every human life at every age under every condition is precious. We know why truth is truth. We know that sin is what explains the brokenness of the world, and we know just how broken it is, starting with ourselves. We know why marriage can only be the union of a man and a woman, and we know why the family best be respected and protected by any sane civilization. We know why right is right and wrong is wrong. We know that life is not meaningless, and that right is not merely socially constructed and up for negotiation. We know that we are responsible creatures—that one day God will judge us for our every thought and deed.

As Russell Kirk reminded us, "wise men know what wicked things are written on the sky."[1] Indeed, we do.

Only the Christian worldview is sufficient to answer the demands of secularization, nor can any other worldview provide the framework for true human flourishing. Silence in this age is not an option—indeed, silence and retreat are tantamount to failure. Believers in Jesus Christ possess the gospel of Jesus Christ, as well as the power of the Holy Spirit. Obedience to Christ demands our faithful stewardship, careful thinking, and wise engagement in the midst of this pressing crisis. Three massive Christian virtues mark our way. As the apostle Paul wrote to the Corinthians: "So now faith, hope, and love abide, these three; but the greatest of these is love" (1 Cor 13:13).

Faith

Christ's people are a people of faith—most centrally, faith in Christ. Without this virtue, the church of Jesus Christ will fall before any challenge. In a secular age, faith is confused. Even some secular people speak of "having faith." But Christians do not have faith in faith, but faith in Christ. Where you find failing churches and denominations, you find a loss of faith in God. Where you find courage, conviction, and steadfastness, you find the people of God with vibrant faith in Christ and his promises. In this secular age, Christians must display faith in at least three ways: faith in God's design, faith in God's Word, and faith in the power of the gospel.

Faith in God's Design

We live in a moment that questions every possible expression of a biblical worldview. We have seen throughout this book the radical transformation of the family and the effects of the sexual revolution on marriage, gender, and sexuality. We expect this from a culture that is secular and moving away from its Christian moral worldview—we do not expect this from churches and denominations that supposedly claim the name of Christ and identify as part of the bride of Christ. Yet, as we have seen, church after church and denomination after denomination has surrendered to this worldview and its demands. These churches have sacrificed biblical fidelity on the altar of cultural relevance; they are willing to discard biblical Christianity in order to be "on the right side of history."

Churches and Christian ministries, however, are on the front line of the cultural challenges. Christians who hold to and teach a biblical vision for marriage and sexuality present a threat to the secular forces seeking to redefine Western civilization. According to the revolutionaries, the Christian worldview is a vestige of an era that is not only fading away, but inherently harmful to humanity and human happiness. This is why the culture places pressure on churches, demanding capitulation (or silence) on social issues like abortion and same-sex marriage. This is why even some candidates for the Democratic nomination have claimed a progressive "Christianity" in an attempt to supplant the historic orthodox faith with a new synthetic religion. It is not Christianity.

Christians, however, must have faith in the creational order of our God and his design for human flourishing. This faith must lead us to express the biblical vision of marriage, to show the glory of biblical manhood and womanhood, and to show this increasingly secularized nation the dignity of human life. Secularization replaces the ontological truth of God with a lie—it replaces biblical truth with a new ideology. Christians must have faith that God's design is not only true and good but the only pathway to human flourishing. If God designed it, it is right. As God himself declared after every day of creation, "It is *good*."

Faith in God's design, however, extends beyond a mere intellectual assent. Faith in God's creational mandates is the very foundation of our worldview and orders all our thinking. Christians, therefore, reveal their faith in God's plan for marriage not only by telling the truth but by living out that truth. As the Bible says in James 2:18: "But someone will say, 'You have faith and I have works.' Show me your faith apart from your works, and I will show you my faith by my works." Christians show their faith in God's design by living faithfully within that design. Our marriages, therefore, must last. Our children should know the Scriptures and the storyline of the Bible. Our families ought to be integrally tied to the local church and experience regular fellowship with the body of Christ. Our oppositions to abortion ought to be met with Christian families adopting and fostering children who are in need.

Faith in God's Word

Where you find faithful churches, you find people committed to the Bible—the infallible, inspired, inerrant Word of God. Throughout this book, we have seen denominations and churches crumble to the Spirit of the Age. Why? Most urgently because they lost faith in the holy Scriptures. When churches open the door to an errant text that is culturally constrained and outdated, those churches are already on the way to a departure from Christian truth.

J. I. Packer, one of the most influential evangelical theologians of our time, once delivered an address entitled "Thirty Years' War: Battle for the Bible." That address was given in 1985—more than thirty years ago. My point is simply this: we are in a long and sustained battle for the full truthfulness and authority of Scripture in the church. In one sense, it has been going on since the dawn of the modern age. The Protestant Reformation enshrined as one of its core principles *sola Scriptura*—an affirmation that the Bible alone is the ultimate source of authority. The "church doctrine of Scripture," as the great theologian B. B. Warfile reminded us, is that "when Scripture speaks, God speaks." Our confidence is that the Bible is

God's Word written. Without the Bible, the church has no authoritative word and no doctrinal order.

The first affirmation the church must make about the Bible is its inspiration. As 2 Peter 1:21 tells us: "For no prophecy was ever produced by the will of man, but men spoke from God as they were carried along by the Holy Spirit." This is a beautiful description of the Bible: divine inspiration. The biblical authors were "carried along by the Holy Spirit," word by word—every word inspired of God and every word fully inspired.

Much of what we have seen in our secular moment is a battle between revolution and revelation. The secular worldview eventually displaced a biblical worldview. Eventually, all claims of divine revelation become meaningless in a secular space. In the academy, there is an ever increasing hostility to any claim of revelation. Elsewhere, claims that the Bible is the Word of God are met with a form of intellectual embarrassment. The church is the final place in a hyper-modern society where the statement "God says" makes any sense at all—but it had better make total sense in the church.

The second affirmation that Christians must make is that the Bible is truthful. This flows from the first affirmation of divine inspiration. If God is the ultimate Author of Scripture, then Scripture is totally true. As Jesus prayed to the Father for the church in John 17:17: "Sanctify them in the truth; your word is truth."

The total truthfulness of Scripture is rightly connected to the Bible's inerrancy—it contains no error. And it never fails, thus it is infallible. The truthfulness of the Bible is crucial to the church standing constant and consistent as the world around us constantly changes its moral compass.

How do we know what marriage is? The Bible defines it. How do we know how to understand male and female? In Matthew 19:4–5, Jesus actually explained both by going back to Genesis 1 and 2: "Have you not read that he who created them from the beginning made them male and female, and said, 'Therefore a man shall leave his father and his mother and hold fast to his wife, and the two shall become one flesh'?" The pattern is revealed, totally trustworthy.

The third affirmation Christians make about the Bible is that it is *sufficient*. It is a sad fact that many Christians never really learned about the sufficiency of Scripture. Put plainly, this means that God has given the churches all we need in order to be faithful. He has told us what we need to know. Furthermore, this means that Christians do not look to any earthly authority to correct or complete that knowledge. This does not mean that Christians learn nothing from modern science or other forms of modern knowledge. It does mean that no external authority provides Christians with knowledge that corrects the Bible or provides any authoritative message.

The sufficiency of Scripture assures the church that we are not waiting for some new word from God or some updated knowledge on matters to which the Bible speaks. We are a people defined by and taught by Christ through the Scriptures.

The other great truth to keep in mind is that God is always faithful to his Word. The church is not at risk of being embarrassed before the world for holding to God's Word. When we look at the choice between revelation or revolution, we are actually recognizing the goodness of God in giving us the Bible—in revealing himself and his ways to us. As Carl F. H. Henry put it so beautifully, God loved us so much that he "forfeited his own personal privacy" in order that we might know and love him.[2]

If we take our stand upon the revelation of God, no revolution—not even a revolution in sex and gender—can confuse us. If we take our stand in any other authority, every revolution will engulf us.

Faith in the Gospel's Power

Faith in the gospel of Jesus Christ means, first of all, faith that Jesus saves. This, put simply, is the most basic fact of Christianity.

The most famous verse of the Scriptures is surely John 3:16: "For God so loved the world, that he gave his only Son, that whoever believes in him should not perish but have eternal life."

As Jesus told Nicodemus, "You must be born again" (v. 7). The good news of the gospel is that salvation comes to all who believe in Christ and repent of their sins. Further, it is by grace we are saved, not by anything we must do or even can do. Salvation comes by the sheer mercy of God.

But it comes at great cost. As the apostle Paul told the Corinthian Christians, the gospel means that Christ died for our sins and that God raised him from the dead, according to the Scriptures. Notice, by the way, the fact that Paul did exactly what we are to do—find out what is true "in accordance with the Scriptures" (1 Cor. 15:3).

Of course, the gospel is the great news that God saves *sinners*, and that is another aspect of biblical truth that we must always keep in mind. Human beings face many problems, but the most basic human problem is something we cannot fix—no therapy can resolve it, nor political platform alleviate. This is crucial for Christians to keep in mind. This keeps us from any cultural or political confusion. Government has a role, but it cannot save.

Christians cannot succumb to any political messianism. The kingdom of Christ will not hide in a political platform.

The Christian worldview underlines the importance of politics and government—rooted in the sovereignty of God and the command to love our neighbor. But the biblical worldview also puts politics in its place. We engage in the political process just like any other dimension of the culture that is under our stewardship—but our ultimate and only hope is in Jesus.

Remember what the apostle Paul wrote in Romans 1:16: "For I am not ashamed of the gospel, for it is the power of God for salvation to everyone who believes." There it is, as clear as can be.

Hope

Hope is not an attribute; it is a conviction. As human beings, we are not capable of holding any attribute with constancy. Hope as an attribute does not last. But our hope is actually our confidence in Christ. *He* is our hope.

With that in mind, what does hope mean for Christians in this life? First of all, it means believing that, in Christ and for his glory, we are able in this world to make a difference. Our lives are not mere accidents of history. God has a purpose for us—here and now.

One of the more interesting verbs in the Old Testament comes from the prophet Jeremiah, who spoke to the people of God even as they were under severe oppression. As God spoke through Jeremiah, he told the people not to lose heart, and to get busy. The instructions to Israel were these: "Build houses and live in them; plant gardens and eat their produce" (Jer. 29:5).

That is amazing and is so incredibly helpful to Christians today. What do we do in the face of a secular age? We build houses and live in them. We get married and have babies and grow families and plant churches and make a difference in the world. One of the saddest and more revealing dimensions of the modern secular worldview is that we see arguments based on climate change that we should have no more babies.

But Christian hope works in another important dimension. It frees us from putting ultimate hope in anything or anyone other than Christ. It even prevents us from expecting final resolution of *any* problem on earth. There are no final victories—there is a realistic understanding of the world as it is. For the Christian, we know both victory and defeat—over and over—and no defeat or victory is final.

National elections come every few years. Every economic plan and tax policy is eventually replaced by another. Judges retire and die. Parties rise and fall.

The Christian worldview can alone explain why all these things are *really* important but never *ultimate*. Our ultimate hope is not in the world but in the world to come. The kingdom of God is coming in its fullness—and Jesus Christ is Lord. In Christ we place our utmost hope, *not* as an attitude but as a conviction.

Remember this: "Now faith is the assurance of things hoped for, the conviction of things not seen" (Heb. 11:1).

Love

The greatest of these is love, Paul wrote. Just as the biblical concept of hope is not an attribute, the biblical concept of love is not sentimentality. Christian love is *substantial*. It takes the form of commitment.

The biblical ordering of love understands that we love because God first loved us. Looking back to John 3:16, we know that our salvation came only because of the sovereign power of God's love—and his love is prior to our love. He loves us long before we love him.

Love took Jesus Christ to the cross. The radical nature of God's love is simply astounding. The first Scripture verse I memorized as a boy was this: "God is love" (1 John 4:8).

But the Bible also tells us that Christians are to love one another. The apostle John even warned that if we do not love our brother and sister in Christ, then we are not the church of God but the children of the devil (1 John 3:10).

Even beyond that, Jesus told us to love our neighbor as ourselves. In that command we find our political and social responsibilities as believers. The greatest of the church fathers, Augustine, taught that Christians should think about two cities, the city of God and the city of man. Each city has its own powerful love. In the city of God, the great love is love of God. In the city of man, it is love of man—of fellow human beings. With such great insight, Augustine showed us that both loves are real, but that only the love of God is eternal. The city of God is populated by those who come to faith in Christ. The city of man includes every human being ever born. The city of God is eternal. The city of man is temporary.

But Augustine's great achievement was to show us how the city of man—the world we know right now—is important to God. God made this world and all things in it. He *loves* this world and all the creatures he has made, especially those made in his image. God wants us to work for good in this world. Christians are told to work for good and for God's glory in this fallen world—because we are commanded to. Our ultimate citizenship is in heaven—the city of God—but we are also now citizens of earthly kingdoms, and not by accident.

This means that Christians *do* have a political responsibility and that politics does matter. Governments matter. Laws matter. Elections matter. Economic policies matter. Everything matters. But how are we to think about this responsibility? What motivates and guides us?

The answer is love.

Jesus set this all out in Matthew 22. When he was asked what the first and greatest commandment was, he answered: "You shall love the Lord your God with all your heart and with all your soul and with all your mind. This is the great and first commandment. And a second is like it: You shall love your neighbor as yourself." Jesus then added, "On these two commandments depend all the Law and the Prophets" (vv. 37–40).

Now you can see the pattern clearly. The city of God is driven by the love of God—undiluted and perfect. The city of man is driven by love of man, real but imperfect. There is more to our biblical understanding. Left on its own, the love of man becomes a dangerous humanism. The greatest rival worldview to biblical Christianity in our day is secular humanism. This form of humanism is idolatrous and corrupted. Humanity is not self-existent nor self-sufficient; and the worship of humanity quickly turns into something deadly.

Secular humanism presents humanity as autonomous and free from all external authority. That leads to disaster.

Christians, however, hold to a different worldview, and are driven by a different motivation. Our motivation is love—love of neighbor. We are called—commanded—to love our neighbor as ourselves. And who is our neighbor? Christ made it clear that every human being is our neighbor.

So, hope gives us the reason to build a home and live in it. Love gives us the reason to build a home for others, for them to live in. Because we love our neighbor, we work for just laws, for righteousness and justice, for the protection of human life, for the good of our neighbors in all things.

This adds so much substance to our responsibility as citizens of the city of man who love our neighbors and love for the glory of God. We can engage in almost every task—economics, politics, elections, entertainment, laws, government, hospitals, adoption agencies, churches, Christian ministries, and just about everything we can imagine—all to the glory of God.

This depends on our stewardship and calling. Ultimately, faith, hope, and love remain, but the greatest of these is love.

The gathering storm is real—and we can see it, and we dare to see it for what it is. But Jesus Christ is Lord, and he promised that the gates of hell shall not prevail over his church. And that is enough.

APPENDIX

The Storm over the Courts

The American system of government, our prized experiment of constitutional government and ordered liberty, depends upon the separation of powers. Fearful of tyranny, the Founders separated the government into the executive, legislative, and judicial branches. Alexander Hamilton famously remarked that the judiciary— the courts—would represent "the least dangerous branch" of government.[1]

Hamilton's assessment seemed to be accurate for a very long time, but more recently the tables have turned. For several decades now, the courts—and the Supreme Court in particular—have taken unto themselves powers that should be in the hand of Congress or the White House. In most cases, the courts have taken up issues that Congress was either unwilling or unable to resolve. In other cases, the judiciary has usurped power for itself.

At the same time, it is important to recognize that the general turn of activism by the courts was primarily driven by political liberals and progressives who were frustrated with the pace of change over many issues. But the liberal activism that marked the federal courts for decades was increasingly checked by conservative presidents who nominated conservative jurists to the federal bench. For that reason, we see many new and troubling developments.

Joshua Jamerson of the *Wall Street Journal* wrote an article that ran with the headline "Democratic Candidates Urged to Back Supreme Court Overhaul." As Jamerson reported,

> Progressive activist groups are pressing Democratic presidential candidates to back proposals for changing the Supreme Court, a move that could draw protests from voters who don't want to upend the staid institution. Pack the Courts, a recently formed group led by San Francisco State University professor Aaron Belkin, is trying to pressure candidates to support an expansion of the high court's membership. Demand Justice, an organization that advocates for a more liberal judiciary, is pushing for a broader set of overhauls: introducing term limits for justices and imposing some form of ethical guidelines, such as making public their tax returns.[2]

Recent changes in the Supreme Court, especially with the appointment of Justices Neil Gorsuch and Brett Kavanaugh, provide the impetus for the rising animus among leading members of the Democratic Party. As Jamerson's article makes clear, some liberals now demand sweeping changes to the structure of the Supreme Court. Why would this be?

Liberals understand the power of the nation's highest court to adjudicate the major issues facing the nation—the legalization of abortion and same-sex marriage did not occur through open debate in the halls of Congress but through a legal decision made by a simple majority of the members of the Supreme Court. What the abortion rights movement and the movement for same-sex marriage could not gain through Congress, they won at the Supreme Court.

Indeed, major culture-shaping shifts on issues like abortion and LGBTQ concerns have not generally come by legislative action but by the courts. Just think of Supreme Court decisions such as *Roe v. Wade* or *Obergefell v. Hodges*. Thus, in many cases, Supreme Court decisions have served as the greatest engine of social change for the liberal moral agenda.

Liberals, however, continue to worry that their influence on the courts is waning. The election of Donald Trump and a Republican majority in the Senate has led to two Supreme Court appointments and to the appointment of 25 percent of the federal judiciary in just the last three years. Presidents George W. Bush and Barack Obama each appointed only two justices to the Supreme Court during their entire eight years in office.

In this light, some Democrats are now arguing that a newly elected Democratic president should "pack" the Supreme Court, adding new seats. Others argue for even more radical moves such as redefining the nation's highest court altogether by replacing life terms with term limits. The deep divide in American politics is reflected in deep division concerning the federal courts.

The competing visions for the Supreme Court center on divergent hermeneutics—different ways of reading a text. In this case, the text is the Constitution of the United States and federal statutes. For decades, more liberal justices and law professors argued for the idea of a "living Constitution" that would evolve with the maturing nation. Conservatives, on the other hand, argued that any text, including the Constitution, should be interpreted in light of the author's original meaning, looking to the actual text at stake. This liberal hermeneutical trend began in the early twentieth century under the leadership of Woodrow Wilson.

Progressives like Wilson, however, believed that the conservative hermeneutical method restricted American progress. They believed that the Constitution itself was too conservative, especially in limiting the powers of the federal government. They saw the way out of their dilemma through redefining how the Constitution was to be read. Progressives posited that the text of the Constitution was living—that the meaning of the text can evolve even if that meaning contradicts the actual words of the document. By the 1950s and '60s, both major political parties bought into this logic of progressive legal interpretation.

Indeed, in 1958, the chief justice of the United States, Earl Warren, authored the majority opinion in the case known as *Trop v. Dulles*. Warren argued in his decision that the Court shall recognize "evolving standards of decency that mark the progress of a maturing society." This succinct statement encapsulates the very ideal of progressivist jurisprudence and morality. He argued that the Supreme Court shall read the Constitution through the "evolving standards," even when this meant that the Court would be inventing new rights or making judgments on the basis of what they felt the Constitution *should* say—not what the text actually states.

The chief justice argued that society moves forward morally, altering its standards of decency and evolving its acceptance of previously held convictions. This argumentation and philosophy drove the Supreme Court and the nation's judiciary from the 1950s and '60s—and it continues even to this day. It is a truly radical judicial philosophy that has altered the moral landscape of American society. In essence, progressives argue that the language of the Constitution must be read through the lens of the present cultural moment. The meaning of its words must be updated to the present needs of contemporary society. They argued that the Court (and often federal courts as well) should update the Constitution by their interpretations. Once again, we see the pattern of more liberal forces seeking to win in cases what they could not win in the course of a public debate in a constitutional republic. The way to change the Constitution is by amendment—not by judicial fiat.

This Constitutional hermeneutical consensus between Republicans and Democrats at the midpoint of the twentieth century led to a series of high court decisions that set the stage for transformative decisions like *Roe v. Wade* in 1973. The modern conservative movement in legal circles emerged as an alternative method of constitutional interpretation—an interpretation of the

Constitution *grounded* in the words, grammar, and intent of the nation's governing document.

But a majority of more progressive justices forged a legal path to abortion (and eventually to same-sex marriage) by finding, first, a constitutional right to privacy—not the actual words of the Constitution but in what Justice William O. Douglas called "penumbras formed by emanations from those guarantees [the Bill of Rights] that help give them life and substance."[3] In other words, Justice Douglas, writing for the Court, just invoked a new right and declared that it should have been in the Bill of Rights—*but it isn't*.

Over the course of just a few years, progressives on the Court ruled in favor of contraception in the *Griswold* case and then in favor of abortion rights. Of course, the US Constitution does not even mention abortion—not even close—but the majority forced it there anyway. Eventually, the same logic would extend to homosexuality and same-sex marriage.

Conservatives do not argue that the Constitution cannot contain such rights, but that it *does not* and *should not*. If the American people wanted to legalize abortion and same-sex marriage, Congress could have legalized them through the legislative process. But there was no political way forward to force the legalization of abortion through Congress in 1973 nor the legalization of same-sex marriage in 2015. So, activists went to the courts, and activist judges gave them what they demanded.

By now it should be clear. Whoever appoints judges to the federal bench and justices to the Supreme Court controls, in large part, the future of the nation.

A Conservative Renaissance

Conservatives, however, responded to the progressive direction of the courts with a new wave of nominees to the federal bench and to the

Supreme Court. These judges represented a constitutional hermeneu-
tic tied directly to the words, intent, and text of the nation's governing
documents. One of the current justices on the Supreme Court, Clarence
Thomas, represents one of the most consistently conservative judges
to sit on the nation's highest court, and his method of interpretation
attracts the concern of many on the left, including the veteran judicial
reporter for the *New York Times*, Adam Liptak.

In March 2019, Liptak authored another article for the *New York
Times* with the headline "Precedent, Meet Clarence Thomas. You
May Not Get Along."[4] Liptak reported, "Justice Clarence Thomas
was busy in February. As usual, he asked no questions during
Supreme Court arguments. But he made up for his silence with
three opinions in eight days that took issue with some of the court's
most prominent precedents."

Justice Thomas raised suspicions over the constitutionality of
New York Times v. Sullivan—a 1964 decision that, as Liptak argued,
"provided the press with broad First Amendment protections
against libel suits brought by public officials. The Sullivan case—
and rulings extending it—Justice Thomas wrote, 'were policy-driven
decisions masquerading as constitutional law.'"

Then, on February 20, Thomas criticized the legalization of
abortion in America through *Roe v. Wade* as "notoriously incorrect."
Liptak summarized Thomas's opinion, stating that *Roe* was "a
product of misguided efforts to identify and protect fundamental
rights under the due process clause of the 14th amendment." Justice
Thomas was directly criticizing the argument of Justice Douglas
about the "penumbras" and "emanations."

The final opinion Thomas wrote in February 2019 "expressed
skepticism about *Gideon v. Wainwright*, the 1963 decision that said
the Sixth Amendment requires the government to provide lawyers
to poor people accused of serious crimes. Justice Thomas wrote that
the Sixth Amendment, as understood by those who drafted and
ratified it, guaranteed only the right to hire a lawyer."

At this point, Liptak intends his article to scandalize his reader. How dare a sitting Supreme Court justice question the legality and legitimacy of three landmark decisions of the United States Supreme Court? Liptak then wrote, "The opinions underscored two distinctive aspects of Justice Thomas's jurisprudence. He tries to unearth the original meaning of the Constitution, and he has no use for precedents that have veered from that original understanding."

What Liptak intended as an indictment against Thomas actually summarized the essence of Thomas's legal philosophy—a philosophy that binds reasoning and arguments to the text of the Constitution. When the Court has deviated from the Constitution, those decisions ought to play no role as an authority for legal precedence. Liptak accuses Thomas of daring to stand on his convictions, for the audacity to mean what he says and say what he means. Indeed, Justice Thomas might hear Liptak's indictment and say, "Guilty as charged!"

Liptak's contention with Justice Thomas stems from his handling of precedents precious to progressives. Precedence has reigned as an important, guiding principle in American legal theory. "*Stare decisis,*" or "stand by things decided," means that prior decisions ought to have an authoritative bearing on present cases before any court. Justice Thomas, as Liptak indicates, does not hold precedents to be more important than the constitutional text—Liptak implies that Justice Thomas is dangerous as a member of the nation's highest court.

But, Justice Thomas does not discount *stare decisis* in full. An erratic court would lose its credibility. He does, however, question the validity of the doctrine if applied to erroneously decided cases that contorted the Constitution and exceeded the boundary of the Supreme Court's authority as a deliberative body entrusted with assessing constitutionality. When the Court departs from this legal principle it begins to legislate from on high—making the will of only five people (a majority of justices) the supreme law of the land.

Justice Thomas, therefore, believes in *privileging* the text of the Constitution even over the text of Supreme Court precedent, some of which he believes has departed from the Constitution's meaning. He calls for a consistent, grounded, and principled reading of the Constitution that binds legal decision to the language and words present within the document itself. Liberal legal interpretation, on the other hand, *invents* rights by reading those rights into the text of the Constitution.

Justice Thomas points to the invalidity of Supreme Court decisions that adopt this kind of legislative, inventive reading of the Constitution—a reading that jettisons the words of the document and imports a political agenda into the text. Those cases, though precedents, have no binding authority because they in no way represent the intended meaning of the Constitution.

If the liberal ideologues wanted abortion or same-sex marriage legal throughout the United States, then that discussion belongs in the halls of Congress or in a Constitutional Convention that brings changes through the expressed will of the people in a new amendment. If we disagree with the Constitution or believe it needs to protect another kind of right, then the Constitution provides a way to accomplish that goal—that way, however, was not a top-down judicial declaration by a simple majority of the justices on the Supreme Court. Justice Thomas, therefore, excoriates Court decisions that invent rights out of thin air, effectively ending a debate that never happened.

We live in a time that rejects authority, that longs to shuffle off the audacious and oppressive claim that texts have meaning—a meaning that we must adhere to and respect. Make no mistake, this is a vital issue for American public life. Either the Constitution has meaning, or it doesn't. Either the law and legal interpretations have grounding in the actual text, or we can just make the text say what we want it to say.

Conservatives began to understand this and responded accordingly. Now, with 2020 on the horizon, the Supreme Court has become one of the most politically charged issues surrounding the presidential election. While conservatives celebrated the confirmations of Gorsuch and Kavanaugh, liberals responded in outrage and have now concentrated their efforts on reversing this conservative resurgence and putting the courts back on a more "progressive" track.

Indeed, if the conservatives panicked in the latter half of the twentieth century, liberals face the same consternation as more and more conservative judges populate the benches of the American judiciary. Liberals are calling for all the major candidates in the Democratic Party to pack the courts and alter major policies such as imposing term limits on justices and increasing the number of seats on the Supreme Court.

Many Democrats, however, understand that changing the laws to try and gain a more liberal court could end up benefiting the conservative agenda. The more tempered and established Democrats grasp the risks involved with changing any laws regarding how many seats are on the Court or imposing term limits on Supreme Court justices—while those laws might give liberals a leg up, those same laws can lead to even more conservatives sitting on the bench.

Despite this risk, the Democratic Party is in an identity crisis. A younger insurgence of liberals has arisen in the rank and file of the Democratic Party—they have come not to continue a reformation but to instigate a revolution.

The moral revolutionaries know that a conservative majority on the Supreme Court exists as the primary barrier to their political and moral agenda. Conservatives now also believe that the courts are the last line of defense against an unfettered, radically liberal agenda. The Court, however, was never intended to endure this level of politicization. So much for the "least dangerous branch."

Conclusion

It says something about our current political moment that both Republicans and Democrats are focused like a laser beam on the Supreme Court and, to a less public extent, the federal judiciary. Millions of voters think of the presidential election with the future of the Supreme Court in mind.

The reason is clear. The Supreme Court and often federal courts now play an outsized role in the nation's public life—a role never intended by the framers. The deep political divide in Congress largely explains the failure of the legislative branch to deal with contentious issues through legislation. An even stronger presidency means that more and more policy is made through administrative channels rather than through legislation. Those who do not like the administrative policy go to the federal courts to seek a block on those policies. Thus, every opening in a federal bench is now a political obsession.

At stake for the left is a series of court decisions that are enshrined in their worldview and have furthered the moral and sexual revolution all around us. The central issue for moral progressives is to protect *Roe v. Wade* at all costs. Consider the confirmation hearings of Justices Neil Gorsuch and Brett Kavanaugh. At almost every excruciating turn (especially during the Kavanaugh hearings) *Roe v. Wade* was cited as the great looming issue.

The obsession over *Roe* makes a great deal of sense when you consider the ongoing fact that if *Roe* were to disappear, there is no way the pro-abortion legislation could get a bill allowing abortion on demand through the Congress. That was Charles Krauthammer's point back in 2015. Even as Americans have grown more liberal on many issues, America is more divided on abortion now than at any point in the nation's history. Krauthammer credited the ultrasound with that fact. While the ultrasound clearly played a major part, revealing the inherent humanity of the unborn child, the effort of the pro-life movement to press the moral case against abortion cannot be dismissed.

The moral revolutionaries also know this—that abortion stands as a central building block of their argument. If the personhood of the unborn child is even recognized in American law, and if *Roe v. Wade* is overturned, their entire line of court decisions is at risk, all the way to same-sex marriage and beyond.

This explains the fanaticism of the left on abortion, and especially on *Roe*. The "right to privacy" invented by the Court in *Griswold* in 1965 led directly to the "right" to abortion in 1973 and the "right" to same-sex marriage in 2015. None of these purported "rights," so cherished by the moral revolutionaries, is remotely mentioned in the Constitution.

Keep in mind that the original frustration among liberals concerning the Constitution was not about moral issues at all, but about constitutional limitations on the growth and power of the federal government. Consider the words of Dean Acheson, US secretary of state from 1949 to 1953; explaining his frustration with the restrictions of the Constitution, he said: "Looking back, the gravest problem I had to deal with was how to steer, in the atomic age, the foreign policy of a world power saddled with the Constitution of a small, eighteenth century farmers' republic."[5] Acheson was simply saying what others had been arguing more indirectly. In their view, the Constitution, with its limited and enumerated power of government, is simply out of date.

Notice an important link here. The progressivists wanted the federal government to escape the Constitution and to take on new powers and authority. Jump to 1965 and the *Griswold* decision and the 1973 *Roe* decision to the 2015 *Obergefell* decision. What is the link? The link is the expanded role of the federal government, now issuing decrees on what the states must accept as policy on issues that the Constitution grants the federal government *no* right to rule.

This brings us back to today, and the challenges faced by Christians in America. With the 2020 elections looming, the future of the Supreme Court and all the federal judiciary will be determined by the election of the president of the United States, who has sole authority to nominate, and the US Senate, which has the sole authority to confirm. Whoever is elected president will nominate all federal judges and, if a seat should open, any justice of the Supreme Court. In the course of the 2020 campaign, both eventual candidates will tell us what kind of judges and justices they will nominate. There is now nowhere for a presidential candidate to hide. So much will depend upon their decision.

For both sides, abortion and *Roe v. Wade* now serve as a test. The Democratic nominee will pledge to appoint only those judges who promise to uphold *Roe*. The Republican nominee will pledge to appoint only those judges who hold to a view of the Constitution that is contrary to *Roe*.

Christians understand that there is more at stake in the storm over the courts—including the future of religious liberty. At no time in our nation's history have the courts been such a focus of attention—and rightfully so.

At the opening of every business day in which the Supreme Court is seated, the Marshall of the Court opens the day by declaring, "God save the United States and his Honorable Court!"

That must be our prayer as well.

ACKNOWLEDGMENTS

I owe a debt to many people whose contributions to my life and work are represented in this book. This debt would extend to all those individuals with whom I have discussed these issues out of common concern, and to the many congregations, colleges, seminaries, and organizations who have invited me to speak on these issues.

Closer to home, I could not do my work without the team of excellent leaders at the Southern Baptist Theological Seminary and Boyce College, including Craig Parker and Matthew Hall as senior vice presidents. Jon Austin, who serves as my chief of staff, is an incredibly steady hand, whose great gifts are essential to the operation of the whole office and team. Each is a servant leader of great dedication, and I am proud to serve with them.

I am particularly thankful for the team of assistants and interns who work with me each day. Cory Higdon serves as director of theological research, and I so appreciate his gift of rare intelligence and eager heart in all that he does, including editing. He constantly prods me to get chapter after chapter to him, and keeps all projects on schedule. Every writer knows that someone has to do this. Few do it with Cory's skill.

Caleb Shaw serves as director of communications and as producer for *The Briefing*. I am thankful for his spirit, dedication, and steady hand as we work through what can only be described as daily chaos.

Caleb would not raise his voice, even if he had to come and tell me that our office had been invaded by communist insurgents. He would simply ask, "What's the plan? Okay, let's go."

Ryan Modisette, the technical engineer for *The Briefing*, is both highly gifted and incredibly flexible—as in often working in the earliest hours of the morning. Never a complaint. I am thankful, and my voice is secure in his hands.

In the office each day, I am surrounded late in the afternoon with an army of the most brilliant, eager, faithful, and joyful interns. They are enormously helpful, even if they make me feel older each passing year. They pass through, on their way to God's calling in their lives. Each leaves a mark, and for each I am thankful. Over the course of this project, interns have included Patrick Vestergaard, Graham Faulkner, Mark Kiefer, David Bunce, Jay Williams, Aaron Woodall, Adam Cole, Anthony Aviles, Jack Cella, and James Power. Much thanks to each of these young men.

Throughout my work of writing, Robert Wolgemuth has been my agent, but more than that, he has been a faithful friend. He knows more about publishing than anyone I know, and he has improved every project. More recently, Andrew Wolgemuth has brought that same spirit and expertise to project after project. Always helpful.

At Thomas Nelson, Webster Younce serves not only as a publisher, but as an advocate and friend and guide. I am thankful for the work we have done together, and for the friendship we have known.

Finally, I want to acknowledge that my every project is enlivened by any interruption from two little grandsons and by every conversation with Riley, Katie, and Christopher. What gifts.

Above all on earth, I want to thank my sweet wife, Mary, whose love and wisdom and fidelity and joy and intelligence are translated into everything I do. After decades of marriage, I cannot calculate the contribution she has made to my life and work and heart. That's the point, isn't it? Love always.

NOTES

Introduction

1. Winston Churchill, vol. 1, *The Gathering Storm, The Second World War* (Boston, MA: H. Mifflin, 1948).
2. "In U.S., Decline of Christianity Continues at Rapid Pace," Pew Research Center, October 17, 2019, https://www.pewforum.org/2019/10/17/in-u-s-decline-of-christianity-continues-at-rapid-pace/.
3. Oliver Roy, *Is Europe Christian?* (London: Hurst and Company, 2019), translated by Cynthia Schoch, 35.
4. Tom Holland, *Dominion: The Making of the Western Mind* (London: Little, Brown, 2019), 517.
5. Cited and summarized by Jurgen Habermas in Jurgen Habermas and Joseph Ratzinger, *The Dialectics of Secularization: On Reason and Religion* (San Francisco: Ignatius, 2006), 21.
6. D. Elton Trueblood, *The Predicament of Modern Man* (New York: Harper & Brothers, 1944), 59.
7. Patrick J. Deneen, *Why Liberalism Failed* (New Haven, CT: Yale University Press, 2018), xiv.
8. Churchill, *The Second World War*, 667.

Chapter 1: The Gathering Storm over Western Civilization

1. Stephen Carter, *The Culture of Disbelief: How American Law and Politics Trivialize Religious Devotion* (New York: Basic Books, 1993), 115.
2. Peter Berger, *The Sacred Canopy: Elements of a Sociological Theory of Religion* (New York: Anchor Books, 1990).

3. Charles Taylor, *A Secular Age* (Cambridge, MA: Belknap Press of Harvard University Press, 2007).

4. Carl F. H. Henry, *God, Revelation, and Authority*, vol. 6, *God Who Stands and Says Part 2* (Wheaton, IL: Crossway, 1999), 454.

5. Carl F. H. Henry, *God, Revelation, and Authority*, vol. 1, *God Who Speaks and Shows, Preliminary Considerations* (Wheaton, IL: Crossway, 1999), 1.

Chapter 2: The Gathering Storm in the Church

1. "Church of Canada May Disappear by 2040, Says New Report," CEP Online, November 18, 2019, https://cep.anglican.ca/church-of -canada-may-disappear-by-2040-says-new-report/.

2. Catherine Porter, "A Canadian Preacher Who Doesn't Believe in God," New York Times, February 1, 2019, https://www.nytimes.com/2019 /02/01/world/canada/grettavosper-reverend-atheism.html.

3. Colin Perkel, "Atheist United Church Minister to Keep Her Job After Reaching Agreement Ahead of 'Heresy Trial'," *Globe and Mail*, November 9, 2018, https://www.theglobeandmail.com/canada /article-atheist-united-church-minister-to-keep-her-job-after -reaching/.

4. Stephanie Armour, "Trump Exempts Christian Social-Services Group From Non-Discrimination Rule," *Wall Street Journal*, January 23, 2019, https://www.wsj.com/articles/trump-exempts-christian-social -services-group-from-non-discrimination-rule-11548282932.

5. Oliver Thomas, "American Churches Must Reject Literalism and Admit We Got It Wrong on Gay People," *USA Today*, April 29, 2019, https://www.usatoday.com/story/opinion/2019/04/29/americanchurch -admit-wrong-gays-lesbians-lgbtq-column/3559756002/.

6. Isaac Stanley-Becker, "'He Knows Better': Pete Buttigieg Has Made Mike Pence His Target, and the Vice President Isn't Pleased," *Washington Post*, April 11, 2019, https://www.washingtonpost.com /nation/2019/04/11/he-knows-better-pete-buttigieg-has-made-mike -pence-his-target-vicepresident-isnt-pleased/.

Chapter 3: The Gathering Storm over Human Life

1. Charles Krauthammer, *The Point of It All: A Lifetime of Great Loves and Endeavors* (New York: Random House, 2018), 117.

2. Mike DeBonis and Felicia Sonmez, "Senate Blocks Bill on Medical Care for Children Born Alive After Attempted Abortion," *Washington Post*,

February 25, 2019, https://www.washingtonpost.com/politics/senate
-blocksbill-on-medical-care-for-children-born-alive-after
-attemptedabortion/2019/02/25/e5d3d4d8-3924-11e9-a06c
-3ec8ed509d15_story.html.

3. Lisa Respers France, "Hollywood Comes Out in Opposition to Georgia's 'Heartbeat' Bill," CNN, March 29, 2019, https://www.cnn.com/2019 /03/29/entertainment/hollywoodgeorgia-heartbeat-bill/index.html.

4. George F. Will, "'Heartbeat Bills' Are Wholesome Provocations in the Abortion Debate," *Washington Post*, May 3, 2019, https://www .washingtonpost.com/opinions/heartbeat-bills-are-wholesome -provocations-in-the-abortion-debate/2019/05/03/6b81f5d8-6cfb-11e9 -a66d-a82d3f3d96d5_story.html.

5. Alan Blinder, "Louisiana Moves to Ban Abortions After a Heartbeat Is Detected," *New York Times*, May 29, 2019, U.S., https://www.nytimes .com/2019/05/29/us/louisiana-abortion-heartbeat-bill.html.

6. Editorial Board, A Woman's Right, *New York Times*, December 28, 2018, https://www.nytimes.com/interactive/2018/12/28/opinion /pregnancy-women-pro-life-abortion.html.

Chapter 4: The Gathering Storm over Marriage

1. Paul A. Murtaugh and Michael G. Schlax, "Reproduction and the Carbon Legacies of Individuals," *Global Environmental Change* 19, no. 1 (2009).

2. Paul Ehrlich, *The Population Bomb* (Cutchogue, NY: Buccaneer Books, 1968).

3. Russell Shorto, "No Babies?—Declining Population in Europe," *New York Times*, June 29, 2008, sec. Magazine, https://www.nytimes.com /2008/06/29/magazine/29Birth-t.html.

4. Anna Louie Sussman, "Opinion | The End of Babies," *New York Times*, November 16, 2019, sec. Opinion, https://www.nytimes.com /interactive/2019/11/16/opinion/sunday/capitalism-children.html.

5. Obergefell v. Hodges, 135 S. Ct. 2584 (2015). See dissenting opinion by Chief Justice John Roberts on pages 3 and 18.

Chapter 5: The Gathering Storm over the Family

1. Christopher Lasch, *Haven in a Heartless World: The Family Besieged* (New York: Basic Books, 1977).

2. Brigitte Berger and Peter L. Berger, *The War over the Family: Capturing the Middle Ground* (Garden City, NY: Anchor Press, 1983).

3. Jeremiah Keenan, "Canadian Court Rules Parents Can't Stop 14-Year -Old From Taking Trans Hormones," *Federalist*, March 1, 2019, https://thefederalist.com/2019/03/01/canadian-court-rules-parents -cant-stop-14-year-old-taking-trans-hormones/.

4. Jill Croteau, "Gay-Straight Alliance Law Challenged at Alberta Court of Appeal," Globalnews.Ca, December 3, 2018, https://globalnews.ca /news/4725221/gay-straight-alliance-bill-24-court-of-appeal-alberta/.

5. Callum Paton, "'Mother' and 'Father' Replaced with 'Parent 1' and 'Parent 2' in French Schools under Same-Sex Amendment," *Newsweek*, February 15, 2019, https://www.newsweek.com/mother-and-father -replaced-parent-1-and-parent-2-french-schools-under-same-1332748.

6. Ruth Woodcraft, "First They Came for the Home Schoolers," *Evangelicals Now*, May 2019, https://www.e-n.org.uk/2019/05/uk-news /first-they-came-for-the-home-schoolers/.

7. Lasch, *Haven in a Heartless World*, 189.

Chapter 6: The Gathering Storm over Gender and Sexuality

1. Moisés Kaufman, "A Dangerous Euphoria," *New York Times*, June 16, 2019, U.S., https://www.nytimes.com/2019/06/16/us/moises-kaufman -stonewall-50.html.

2. Kaufman, "A Dangerous Euphoria."

3. Kaufman, "A Dangerous Euphoria."

4. Jeremy Allen, "Chasing the L.G.B.T.Q. Millennial American Dream," *New York Times*, June 13, 2019, U.S., https://www.nytimes .com/2019/06/13/us/lgbtq-millennial-marriage.html.

5. Nathaniel Frank, "A Match Made in Heaven," *Washington Post*, June 21, 2019, https://www.washingtonpost.com/news/posteverything /wp/2019/06/21/feature/a-match-made-in-heaven/.

6. Martina Navratilova, "The Rules on Trans Athletes Reward Cheats and Punish the Innocent," February 17, 2019, Comment, https://www .thetimes.co.uk/article/the-rules-on-trans-athletes-reward-cheats-and -punish-the-innocent-klsrq6h3x.

7. Amy Harmon, "Which Box Do You Check? Some States Are Offering a Nonbinary Option," *New York Times*, May 29, 2019, U.S., https://www .nytimes.com/2019/05/29/us/nonbinary-drivers-licenses.html.

8. Daniel Bergner, "The Struggles of Rejecting the Gender Binary," *New*

York Times, June 4, 2019, Magazine, https://www.nytimes.com /2019/06/04/magazine/gender-nonbinary.html.

9. Revoice, "Vision," https://revoice.us/about/our-mission-and-vision/.

10. Revoice, "Vision," https://revoice.us/about/our-mission-and-vision/.

11. Revoice, "Creation and Design," https://revoice.us/about /our-beliefs/statements-of-conviction/statement-on-sexual -ethics-and-christian-obedience/.

12. Mark Galli, "Revoice's Founder Answers the LGBT Conference's Critics," *Christianity Today*, July 25, 2018, https://www .christianitytoday.com/ct/2018/july-web-only/revoices -founder-answers-lgbt-conferences-critics.html.

13. Gregory Coles, *Single, Gay, Christian* (Downers Grove, IL: InterVarsity Press, 2017), 110.

14. Denny Burk and Heath Lambert, *Transforming Homosexuality: What the Bible Says About Sexual Orientation and Change* (Phillipsburg, NJ: P&R Publishing, 2015).

15. Denny Burk and Rosaria Butterfield, "Learning to Hate Our Sin Without Hating Ourselves," *Public Discourse*, July 4, 2018, https://www .thepublicdiscourse.com/2018/07/22066/.

16. Wesley Hill, *Spiritual Friendship: Finding Love in the Church as a Celibate Gay Christian* (Grand Rapids: Brazos, 2015), 78.

17. Nate Collins, *All but Invisible: Exploring Identity Questions at the Intersections of Faith, Gender, and Sexuality* (Grand Rapids: Zondervan, 2017).

Chapter 7: The Gathering Generational Storm

1. Christian Smith, *Soul Searching: The Religious and Spiritual Lives of American Teenagers* (New York: Oxford University Press, 2005), 3.

2. Christian Smith, *Souls in Transition: The Religious and Spiritual Lives of Emerging Adults* (New York: Oxford University Press, 2009), 4.

3. Smith, *Souls in Transition*, 45–46.

4. Smith, 12.

5. Smith, 30.

6. Smith, 84.

7. Smith, 155.

8. James Davison Hunter, *Evangelicalism: The Coming Generation* (Chicago: University of Chicago Press, 1987), 34.

9. Gerald F. Seib, "Cradles, Pews and the Societal Shifts Coming

to Politics," *Wall Street Journal*, June 24, 2019, Politics, https://www
.wsj.com/articles/cradles-pews-and-the-societal-shifts-coming
-to-politics-11561382477.

10. Jeffrey M. Jones, "U.S. Church Membership Down Sharply in Past Two
Decades," April 18, 2019, Gallup.com, https://news.gallup.com
/poll/248837/church-membership-down-sharply-past-two-decades
.aspx.

11. The Editorial Board, "America's Millennial Baby Bust," *Wall Street
Journal*, May 28, 2019, Opinion, https://www.wsj.com/articles
/americas-millennial-baby-bust-11559086198.

12. Roni Caryn Rabin, "Put a Ring on It? Millennial Couples Are in No
Hurry," *New York Times*, May 29, 2018, Well, https://www
.nytimes.com/2018/05/29/well/mind/millennials-love-marriage
-sex-relationships-dating.html.

13. David Brooks, "The Coming G.O.P. Apocalypse," *New York Times*,
June 3, 2019, Opinion, https://www.nytimes.com/2019/06/03/opinion
/republicans-generation-gap.html.

Chapter 8: The Gathering Storm and the Engines of Culture

1. Alvin and Hiedi Toffler, *Future Shock* (New York: Random House,
1970).

2. Megan Townsend, "GLAAD's 'Where We Are on TV' Report Shows
Television Telling More LGBTQ Stories Than Ever," glaad.org,
September 25, 2018, https://www.glaad.org/blog/glaads-where-we-are
-tv-report-shows-television-telling-more-lgbtq-stories-ever.

3. Jessica Shortall, "Why Many Businesses Are Becoming More Vocal in
Support of LGBTQ Rights," *Harvard Business Review*, March 7, 2019,
https://hbr.org/2019/03/why-many-businesses-are-becoming-more
-vocal-in-support-of-lgbtq-rights.

4. Mike Isaac and Kevin Roose, "Facebook Bars Alex Jones, Louis
Farrakhan and Others from Its Services," *New York Times*, May 2, 2019,
Technology, https://www.nytimes.com/2019/05/02/technology
/facebook-alex-jones-louis-farrakhan-ban.html.

5. Bret Stephens, "Facebook's Unintended Consequence," *New York
Times*, May 3, 2019, Opinion, https://www.nytimes.com/2019/05/03
/opinion/facebook-free-speech.html.

6. Isaac and Roose, "Facebook."

7. "Charles Murray on Elites" *Inside Higher Ed*, September 2, 2008,

https://www.insidehighered.com/blogs/university-diaries
/charles-murray-elites.

8. Bill Savage, "Lessons Learned," *Stranger,* June 9, 2005, https://www
.thestranger.com/seattle/lessons-learned/Content?oid=21744.

Chapter 9: The Gathering Storm over Religious Liberty

1. Edwin Meese, *Major Policy Statements of the Attorney General, Edwin Meese III, 1985–1988* (Ann Arbor: University of Michigan Library, 1989), 168.

2. Billy Hallowell, "U.S. Civil Rights Commission Chairman Says Religious Freedoms 'Stand for Nothing Except Hypocrisy,'" DeseretNews.com, September 14, 2016, https://www.deseretnews
.com/article/865662326/US-Civil-Rights-Commission-chairman-says
-religious-freedoms-stand-for-nothing-except-hypocrisy.html.

3. Michael McConnell, "The Problem of Singling Out Religion," *DePaul Law Review* 50, no. 1 (2000): 43–44.

4. Marc D. Stern, "Same-Sex Marriage and the Churches," in *Same-Sex Marriage and Religious Liberty: Emerging Conflicts,* eds. Douglas Laycock, Anthony R. Picarello, and Robin Fretwell Wilson (Lanham, MD: Rowman & Littlefield, 2008), 1.

5. Stern, "Same-Sex Marriage and the Churches," 57.

6. Chai R. Feldblum, "Moral Conflict and Conflicting Liberties," in *Same-Sex Marriage and Religious Liberty: Emerging Conflicts,* eds. Douglas Laycock, Anthony R. Picarello, and Robin Fretwell Wilson (Lanham, MD: Rowman & Littlefield, 2008), 124–125.

7. Feldblum, "Moral Conflict and Conflicting Liberties," 125.

8. Maggie Gallagher, "On Chai Feldblum's Claim That I Misquoted Her," *National Review* (blog), October 28, 2014, https://www.nationalreview
.com/corner/chai-feldblums-claim-i-misquoted-her-maggie-gallagher/.

9. Erasmus, "A Court Ruling Makes It Harder for Faith-Based Employers to Discriminate," *Economist,* April 26, 2018, https://www.economist
.com/erasmus/2018/04/26/a-court-ruling-makes-it-harder-for-faith
-based-employers-to-discriminate.

10. "Equality in America Town Hall with Beto O'Rourke (D), Presidential Candidate," CNN, Transcript, October 10, 2019, http://transcripts.cnn
.com/TRANSCRIPTS/1910/10/se.06.html.

11. Michael McGough, "Opinion: Beto O'Rourke's 'Church Tax' Idea Plays into the Conservative Narrative about Same-Sex Marriage," *Los Angeles*

Times, October 11, 2019, https://www.latimes.com/opinion
/story/2019-10-11/beto-orourke-church-tax-same-sex-marriage-lgbtq.

12. Mark Tushnet, "Abandoning Defensive Crouch Liberal
Constitutionalism," Balkinization, May 6, 2016, https://balkin.blogspot
.com/2016/05/abandoning-defensive-crouch-liberal.html.

13. Todd J. Gillman, "Trump Calls Beto O'Rourke 'Wacko' for Threat to
Revoke Tax-Exempt Status of Religious Groups That Oppose Same-Sex
Marriage," *Dallas News*, October 14, 2019, https://www.dallasnews
.com/news/politics/2019/10/11/beto-orourke-says-hed-revoke-tax
-exempt-status-of-religious-groups-that-oppose-same-sex-marriage/.

14. Frank Bruni, "Religious Liberty, Bigotry and Gays," *New York Times*,
January 10, 2015, Opinion, https://www.nytimes.com/2015/01/11
/opinion/sunday/frank-bruni-religious-liberty-bigotry-and-gays.html.

Conclusion

1. Russell Kirk, *The Wise Men Know What Wicked Things Are Written on
the Sky* (Washington, DC: New York: Regnery Gateway; Distributed by
Kampmann, 1987).

2. Carl F. H. Henry, *God, Revelation, and Authority, Vol 3: The God Who
Speaks and Shows* (Wheaton, IL: Crossway, 1999), 405.

Appendix

1. *The Federalist Papers* No. 78.

2. Joshua Jamerson, "Democratic Candidates Urged to Back Supreme
Court Overhaul," *Wall Street Journal*, March 25, 2019, sec. Politics,
https://www.wsj.com/articles/democratic-presidential-candidates-face
-calls-to-embrace-supreme-court-overhaul-11553518800.

3. *Griswold v. Connecticut*, 381 U.S. 479 (1965). See the majority decision.

4. Adam Liptak, "Precedent, Meet Clarence Thomas. You May Not Get
Along.," *New York Times*, March 4, 2019, U.S., https://www.nytimes
.com/2019/03/04/us/politics/clarence-thomas-supreme-court
-precedent.html.

5. As cited in Erik von Kuenelt-Leddhin, *The Intelligent American's Guide
to Europe* (New Rochelle, NY: Arlington House, 1979), 407.

ABOUT THE AUTHOR

R. Albert Mohler Jr. has been called "one of America's most influential evangelicals" (*Economist*) and the "reigning intellectual of the evangelical movement" (Time.com). The president of the Southern Baptist Theological Seminary, he writes a popular blog and a regular commentary, available at AlbertMohler.com, and hosts two podcasts: *The Briefing* and *Thinking in Public*. He is the author of many books, including *The Apostles' Creed, We Cannot Be Silent,* and *The Prayer That Turns the World Upside Down,* and has appeared in the *New York Times,* the *Wall Street Journal, USA Today,* and on programs such as NBC's *Today,* ABC's *Good Morning America,* and *PBS NewsHour with Jim Lehrer.* He and his wife, Mary, live in Louisville, Kentucky.